Evolution of the Sustainable Huwoman

Chapter 18

Nicola Sage Gardner

Sea Dream Press

VICTORIA, AUSTRALIA

First published in 2024

This body of work is written and produced by a living natural native being of the Earth and is non-AI. It is based on the author's experiences, philosophies and observations.

All inquiries should be made to the author. Nonagone9@yahoo.com
National Library of Australia Cataloguing-in-Publication entry: XXX
Cover artwork/design: Nicola Sage Gardner
Layout and production: Sea Dream Press – **seadreampress.com.au**
Editing: Tricia Szirom, Leanda Michelle and Marinda Wilkinson

Disclaimer:
The material in this publication is of the nature of general comment only and does not represent professional advice. It is not intended to provide specific guidance for particular circumstances and it should not be relied on as the basis for any decision to take action or not take action on any matter which it covers. Readers should obtain professional advice where appropriate, before making any such decision. To the maximum extent permitted by law, the author and publisher disclaim all responsibility and liability to any person, arising directly or indirectly from any person taking or not taking action based on the information in this publication.

Sustainable Huwoman/Nicola Sage Gardner. – 1st ed.
ISBN 978-0-646-89001-2

TESTIMONIALS

CRAP and the huwoman: Sci-fi madness or trenchant critique of the modern world? Whatever your opinion, I challenge you not to find nuggets of gold in this exuberant reimaging of the human condition and destiny.

- Richard Kentwell

It is always a refreshing thing to be lead through the ideas of another that take you to unexpected places. Original work from a brave and generous writer that is exciting to read. Good luck

- Allan Withmore

Earth is changing rapidly, yet are we aware of what we are creating? At the heart of Nicola Sage Gardner's deep dive into recreating our Earth is awareness of the impact we as a population have had on the planet and each other from viewing negative images introduced by what Nicola describes as the 'CRAP' system. She invites us to explore an in-depth, curious alternative to human life on our planet and shines a spotlight on a positive future for all living beings. There is never a more poignant time to dream into our reality the world we truly want for future generations. Nicola's dream is one blueprint for creation; what will yours be?

- Leanda Michelle

Climate breakdown and the rapid unravelling of our living planet are upon us. Finding a way to the other side and restoring our bio-

sphere will require humanity to release ourselves from many entrenched and destructive patterns that led us to the brink. We need to harness the best of our potential – collaboration, problem-solving, empathy, innovation, fearlessness, compassion and connection with ourselves, each other, and our natural world. Nicola Sage Gardner takes us on an exploration of an alternate way of being – the Huwoman – her imaginary archetype for our evolved future descendant who embodies many of the attributes humanity will need to lean into if we are going to survive and thrive in the future.

- Brendan Condon

I loved how this book opened my mind to a completely different way of thinking about so many things. Nicola has put into words many deep-buried inklings and knowing's from within that I have felt but have not previously understood. Definitely a book to read, reflect upon and read again. Life-changing and potential world-changing if we are brave enough to care.

- Marinda Wilkinson

ACKNOWLEDGEMENTS

I would like to acknowledge those of us who have crossed paths, touched each other's lives, whose paths I may still cross, and to the many people who may not have been introduced to this book's concepts. May you be inspired to create a huwoman paradigm.

A very special thanks to my dear friend Tricia Szirom who is the huwoman embodiment of kindness, for her support, encouragement and her words on the back cover. To Jane Moore for her friendship, love and support. To Kay Raymer for her wisdom and many years of guidance when as a young woman I was searching.

To Mum and Yaya for being Mum and Yaya. To Annie Irish for 50 years of friendship. To Jane Chandler, Deb Peck, Priscilla Manthey and Shannon Mc Millan for their friendship. To Aldyth and Ewan Tyler and their clan for always making me feel like family.

Many thanks to the kind and generous people in my neighbourhood and neighbouring communities – the Numbsculls, the food collective, the ethics group and the neighbourhood food swap.

A special thanks to Liz Jacobs, Debbie Williams, Michael Nugent, Richard Kentwell, Jim Stone, Pat Wishart and Angela Wishart for their care and support.

To Aileen Venning, Jessica Harrison, Allan Withmore, Michael Milnes, Neil Smith, George Villella, thank you all for looking out for me and being part of a caring community.

To Leanda Michelle for taking me to the first stages with editing and production and to Marinda Wilkinson for the final stages of the editing process.

To the original ancestors of this land, thank you for hearing my song, I am grateful for your passage – may you continue to hold the spirit of this land.

Contents

INTRODUCTION

So, who are we? Who or what have we become? I don't recognise us anymore.

I have taken the challenge from my first book, *Questions from a Sometimes Philosopher Looking for Utopia*, to explore the depths of what my utopia may look like and to expose the many levels of present underlying human psychology – the psychology of us.

In brief, this book (with the aid of the power of imagination) is exploring and redesigning the human animal species to evolve into the highly sophisticated huwoman. The huwoman's physical body is more adept to survival in the elements and is highly attuned to her senses, allowing her to exist in harmony with her environment, while at the same time her sophistication, intelligence and understanding is more evolved than that of the present human, allowing her access to that which does not only reside in physical matter but in the ethereal plane as well.

She is a future and necessary evolution of the human species born with a highly evolved sense of wisdom, knowing and understanding that unity within and without are synonymous with harmonious existence. She connects both the physical and the non-physical worlds, loses the arrogance of ego, violence and greed and instead gains a humble humility towards all which surrounds her whether in physical form or ethereal in shape.

Even though the concepts expressed are at times esoteric and will be unimaginable to some people, it is important to understand and know that everything is possibility and we create our possibilities with our thoughts, words and actions. We created and made our present system possible and there is no reason why we can't create another possibility, one based on peace, kindness and respect. A much more desirable future is what this book offers.

I have written this book because it is time that we start acting from a fresh perspective and prepare for a totally new way of thinking – beyond the fantasy world of what can be, to the imagination of endless possibilities. At the very least, to allow the concepts of this book to bring new thinking and possibilities into the thoughtlessly destructive reality of our present paradigm. To create this highly evolved person and culture, it is necessary to embody her ethos of kindness, caring and peaceful survival with our imaginative minds, thoughts and actions.

As an exploration into a new world, one that we have the opportunity to create, this book comes with intertwined wisdom from a caring perspective. It does not make for a quick or light read and as such, it is best read right through and may need to be read multiple times allowing for regular pause to reflect as part of the reading process.

To encourage reflection, quotes (such as the one below) are dotted throughout – a collection of my symmetry of words that act as a laser beam, to hone in on and consider, as you open your mind to the possibility of what our future may hold.

The war began the moment we started wearing shoes.

PART ONE

THE EVOLUTION OF THE HUMAN RACE TO A NEW SPECIES: THE HUWOMAN

Maybe you will resonate with the huwoman species. Maybe you will ridicule the possibility. It is offered as an alternative to our present-day life and is an exercise in the release and opening of our imagination. To open one's imagination is to remove the most thwarting aspect, that of judgement. An open mind is a mind without judgement. A judgemental mind is narrow, reactive and nonreceptive. Opinions are based on a belief system and are also judgemental, whereas philosophies are based on observation, understanding and connecting the observations.

To redirect our present trajectory of madness and annihilation we must take charge of our own destiny from an imaginative evolutionary aspect. To do this we need to understand not only the relationship between ourselves, the universe and serendipity, but also the importance of the trinity, the astral and the ethereal realms, as a way of creating our necessary huwoman evolution.

The huwoman described in this book is deep inside us all. We know it intuitively, but we don't know how to access her because we are all entrapped women and men in the present ruling trinity of capitalism, religion and patriarchy (the 'CRAP' system). The CRAP system prefers to self-destruct rather than face itself and take a deep look at itself, especially in the disrespectful destruction it continues to show and create towards our planet for monetary goals and at any cost.

The CRAP system is a system based on fear, control and fantasy – fear of women is especially prevalent in this system, and for both men and women, fear of the huwoman who lives within us all. Our species, phenotypically speaking, is female in origin and we must all morph back into her for a future in harmony.

By the wonders of the creative force of the organic world (of which we are all made) the possibilities suggested for the evolvement of the huwoman, have been used by other species on this amazingly and imaginatively structured planet. All that needs to be done in this evolution is to imagine the possibility of it in one person.

In our present ego-based scientific culture we believe that knowledge is measurable and liberating, however knowledge can be restricting and a hindrance to the imagination. When we think we are knowledgeable then it becomes impossible to create beyond knowledge, because we do not believe that anything beyond knowledge is possible or exists. We then exclude what is beyond knowledge and the endless possibilities of the imagination to create knowingly beyond belief.

Knowing is awareness.
Knowledge is fabrication.

The ability to imagine and create beyond our present limited paradigm of what we believe is possible is paramount to our survival – and I don't mean through man-made 'science technology'. Look around you. We have been made, and everything organic on this planet and in the universe has been created, by the organic world. I call this creative energy nature's 'organic technology'. It happened without any help from science technology. Science technology seems amazing and progressive in the short term but is ultimately unsustainable in the long term. Science technology in the way it is heading is detrimental to our psychological wellbeing and to future physical existence. It is moving at an unprecedent speed, with no pause to reflect on the consequences of its trajectory and the madness it is creating.

Imagination is an impulse of organic technology and for survival all species have and need this imaginative and creative impulse to be able to evolve and continue to interact with the changing environment around them – otherwise they would cease to exist.

Our species has been seduced by the power of the fantasy of the CRAP system and instead of evolving by imagination to adapt to the organic environment, we are evolving to adapt to the fantasies of our artificially created environment, the consequences being that we will eventually cease to exist. (More on imagination and fantasy to come.)

One example is, that due to our modern highly processed food diets and lifestyles, our jaws and our oral cavities are shrinking. The consequences of smaller jaws and more mouth breathing has led to a rise in the need for orthodontic treatment and the removal of wisdom teeth, as well as other side effects such as obstructive sleep apnoea. It seems, these days, that being fitted with braces and wearing retainers is now a late childhood rite of passage.

Our lifestyle and diet (among other things) combined with the overuse of personal technological devices and reliance on technology, is already having an effect on the evolution of the human body from a physical, mental and psychological perspective.

If we start with the already existing human form and do a little organic technology evolutionary adjustment (with our imagination to start with) we could end up with a huwoman who can live in all sorts of environments. Gaia help us, we will need it at the rate our hungry capitalist economy is carving up the environment to line its pockets. Capitalism encourages population growth, making the need to house, feed and clothe our growing human population lucrative, but ultimately unsustainable and anti-life.

We must reduce our population, reconnect with the earth our home and stop the destructive tampering of the Earth in the delusional belief that we are improving ourselves.

We can start doing this by imagining beyond our primordial belief of duality, moving to become the trinity inside, in tune with the energy of the planet and the universe itself. Finding the trinity inside is the point of inner balance where the conflict of duality is resolved with a unifying third option. (More on the trinity to come.)

What makes this future version of our species sustainable is that she does not need to eat, drink or wear clothing, but instead gains her energy from the natural light of the sun, moon and stars.

As the huwoman does not need to eat or drink, she will move beyond the primordial paradigm of our present evolution, to become non-predatory, non-territorial, peaceful in nature and connected to a close intergenerational family-type of community where the responsibility for the rearing and nurturing of children (and each other) belongs to everyone.

Since this evolutionary species in make-up is non-predatory, it is therefore non-violent and respectful. As difficult as this may seem in our separating and competitive duality paradigm, one has to be able to understand and imagine this evolution from a **non-violent** perspective. This peaceful species also has the confidence of boldness and courage as part of her make-up.

I have called this evolution of our species 'Hu-wo/man' because she is a modified version of our present evolution and inclusive of the present separation of the sexes. I am merging the duality into a blend of the present positive female and male attributes to make a third – a trinity within – to unify our species.

This merging and individualising of the separation between us into a third entity, acts as a harmonious singularity for a sustainable existence.

This evolution is not done by tampering with science technology but by the tempering time of organic technology and biological biodiversity. We only need look around us to observe that the natural technology of nature is everywhere. Look at the amazing evolutions and the diversity of species on this planet alone; created with no help from our present capitalist ego-based scientific technology.

Our present human is in the process of devolution and contrary to popular belief, imaginative awareness plays a major part. Therefore, if we do not start to imagine our evolution from tempering time, that is the natural organic environmental evolution, as opposed to scientific tampering, there is no doubt that our species will become extinct or close to. One doesn't need to be Einstein to see this become our reality.

∞

Three things separate us from other species: we have the ability to act beyond our biology, we have the ability to be conceptual and we have evolved into a physical body shape which allows us to create and materialise our concepts and due to this, we are prone to create with the indulgences of our fantasies rather than with the wisdom of our imagination.

If we cannot imagine our future evolution, then we are on the road to become extinct like the many species we have played a major part in driving to extinction due to our lack of imagination for survival. Every possibility I suggest for the huwoman has already been imagined and is already functioning in other species known to us on earth making this a real possibility. I find it mind-blowing that we evolved from fish and some species of dinosaurs became birds. With that in mind, it is not a huge step over time to go from human to huwoman.

The huwoman, being non-predatory, will eliminate her lust for violence and place her energy in peaceful, compassionate and creative pursuits. Can you imagine what it would be like to walk on the Earth without fear of violence and personal harm? Most women and few men would understand this. If we cannot imagine peace then we cannot create it.

The merging of our present duality will temper and balance our present oppositional play of the feminine and masculine.

Even if one can't imagine the huwoman, one can at least act to become more like her. We can do this by encompassing the duality within ourselves to make an integrated third and balanced entity, which creates another reality that frees us from the chains of our current limitations in present madness.

It is possible for humans to move beyond the current limitations of what we are in our male/female duality to become a new advanced species, the huwoman. If we don't take the next evolutionary step with our imagination, thoughts and actions to change our psychology of behaviour, we will surely become extinct.

We are heading for a turbulent, conflicting, explosive and possibly apocalyptic time created by us. You may say apocalyptic times have come and gone before on this planet and they have been instrumental in creating evolution. Only this time we are leaving so much inorganic material behind that I don't even know how our planet will absorb it. Burning, burying and later regurgitating it through the mouth of her volcanoes may be her only option to cleanse herself from the toxic pollution we have created.

The toxicity of burning and regurgitating inorganic material is a problem in itself – making the atmosphere not only unpleasant but unlivable. I have no idea how our planet will deal with the amount of plastic and toxins in her ocean and on her land, and I have no idea how our planet will regenerate herself for habitable life again. At least the evolution of the huwoman is in with a better chance.

Unfortunately, we are 8 billion in population, and growing, and there are no signs of stopping this apocalyptic trajectory, which on its path will cause unnecessary suffering and irreparable damage, not only to the generations of humanity to come, but to the planet our home.

If we act now to reduce our population, reduce our waste and work together to reduce the effects of our trajectory, we may have a chance to create the age of wisdom and end the age of stupidity created by the CRAP system.

Yes, it's all too hard and we don't want to think about it, let alone take any action to save ourselves. It is not uncommon that when we are made aware of the consequences of our seemingly harmless actions, rather than take note and start making the life-giving changes necessary for ourselves and our planet, instead of listening we become angry. It has now become our belief system that it is our right to do whatever we want and how dare anyone tell us how to live. That reaction is the ultimate in disconnection from our life-giving environment – and yet we still cannot see the necessity nor act to make the necessary changes for our future. Who are we? What have we become?

As usual we will wait until it's too late and act in reaction like victims following the often unwise decisions made out of desperation by our scientists, governments and the faceless men who control our economy.

The more we destroy our environment, the more science we invent to try to rectify our fuck-ups, making us feel like we are doing something about our predicament and that we are in good hands. Round and round we go in this delusion, like bull terriers chasing the fantasies of our missing tails and bereft of morals in the chase.

In the patriarchal system of logic, we believe that only something which is measurable is real. This type of exclusive and reductionist reality limits the observational possibilities of a reality beyond measurement.

I dare you as women and men to imagine yourselves removed from the fantasy of the patriarchal world and create a reality beyond its restrictive measurable reality.

ODE TO THE HUWOMANKIND

To the huwoman of my imagination, may you come to life and take us to an evolution where kindness is kindred and kindred is connected and connected is who we are.

As human we have lost connection and our humanity. Take us from this disconnection to the loving place where we belong. Through you may we evolve to become the huwoman we truly are.

Who is the huwoman outside our present duality?

The huwoman is made up of a combination of our present female and male separate entities creating a third: the hu/wo/man. The word unpacked encompasses our duality, brings it together and creates a new species in unity and harmony.

The word hu/man is exclusive of the other half of our species and Hu/wo/man is inclusive of both. Likewise, the word s/he is inclusive of both.

The huwoman, like any independent woman not partnered, is not bound by the obligation which comes from having to trade and compromise for exclusive partnership rights to reproduce. Like any independent woman in her own power, the huwoman will generally have many friends and companionships which are not exclusive but meet her different levels of interests and enjoyments. She is free and unbound by the cultural limitations imposed towards women and men in our present culture's idea of society and what we all agree and act upon to make our reality – in this case the CRAP system.

The huwoman is not caught up in our present reality. She is an independent woman, and like any independent woman, in the true sense of communion she creates friendships, companionships and shares with them in pleasure rather than by the obligation of exclusivity and attachments rules. The huwoman is fully in her own awareness so that she can walk alongside others in self-awareness, without attachment and the need to find security exclusively in someone else, which (generally) has many pitfalls for the degree of happiness it really provides.

Balance and clarity come from being in one's own power to trust in oneself, removing the need for attachments. Finding security and meaning in another creates servitude and disconnection in the trying to connect.

The huwoman is open to express her many aspects with those she connects with and who are part of her liberating and expansive community made of kindness, peace and harmony.

She has the sensibility of a woman and the drive of masculine energy to create in healthy connection with others and with her environment, knowing that all is sacred and to be cherished and respected to create harmony.

What is the huwoman's purpose and how does she create?

Does the huwoman need a purpose? And do we, in our present form of duality, have a purpose?

The huwoman is the combination of the best qualities and characteristics of what we currently describe as female and male. She moves us beyond duality into balance. Phenotypically speaking, we as a species are female in origin and the huwoman returns us to our origins.

The huwoman is the natural evolution after the experience of a duality paradigm because the duality we are in is like being in the teenage years of evolution and the huwoman will bring us in balance and take us to the next phase of evolution. The evolvement of the huwoman also contributes to the existence and expansion of the universal consciousness, which needs the continual creation of animated physical forms.

How can one create without taking or reshaping from something or someone else? Is that even possible? Would the huwoman create from her imagination and in the imagination realm from a space of causing no harm to the animate or inanimate?

The purpose of the huwoman is to explore and interact with the physical world around her, be with her kin, and share in mentoring children. Rather than create by destroying or reshaping the physical, from a child she is taught to create her imaginings in her dream world with the intensity and complexity of imagery that dreams in her sleep are capable of. In this way she creates from and in virtual imagination without causing any harm nor at the expense of other organic life, animate or inanimate.

The huwoman in her early years is taught to live and enjoy the sensual world of the physical, to imagine in the ethereal world of the astral and create her imaginings in the world of the dream. From an early age the huwoman child is guided in the art of seeing through the veil of the astral to enter a world of a different kind.

As an adult she is physically active. Her daily life consists of using her open eyes for the pleasure of physical navigation; the sight behind closed eyes for the pleasure of navigating the astral plane of ethereal light; and the sight during sleep for navigating and experiencing the pleasure of her imaginings in ethereal and virtual time. In ancient cultures the shawoman and shaman's ability to create in the virtual was a reality. There are so very few cultures of sha-people left on our planet of destruction. What a tragedy to have lost the world of the sha-people to the limitations of ego-based science and technology and its destructive trajectory.

Why can't we accept that organic technology has its own virtual reality, not reliant on destructive methods and waiting to be tapped into? And yet, we believe in the artificial intelligence being created in the inorganic destructive technology of the present to experience the virtual reality of someone else's fantasies.

Live in the physical, create with the ethereal light in the astral, experience creation in the virtual realm of the dream; in this way life has no need to destroy nor worship another.

When I looked up online the purpose of humans on earth, there were in excess of 445,000,000 results. The gist of them was from the western religion viewpoint and as follows:

- To serve our creator (our creator being a male God)
- To live in harmony with His moral principle (the conceptual duality of right and wrong)
- To develop our personal talents which of course God has endowed upon us for the benefits of the global society (we've fucked that one up). There is no society without a healthy planet
- He also created humans from love for the purpose of sharing that love towards Him – (what vanity!) and each other (our present interpretation of love is emotional neediness and often the antithesis of selfless universal love)
- When God created humans, He gave them work as a purpose so that they might experience the goodness of God and reflect His image in the way we care for the world and for each other (we've definitely fucked that up!).

Our present human images of the Earth and the way we behave towards her are scary indeed. There is little goodness there – just rape, pillage and reap for financial gain!

Does that mean that we are reflecting God not only in His image but also in our image? And are we not the same image? Does this mean that divinity in our ungodly paradigm is maleness and in the name of the father and of the son? How can that even be remotely so when there is also woman? Therefore, in the correct image of God there must also be a woman – where is she?

Hang on a minute… the woman! She's not important, she is the servant of God and man, the maid. Just because she can create God's children in his image makes her part of the fauna and therefore, she must be controlled and we have been given that right by our male God to do so.

With all that moral religion drummed into us (which has highly influenced our culture and our learning) it is not surprising that the CRAP system has emerged and is justified. This system operates in the duality of good and evil and has created humans primarily looking after themselves. Even when humans are charitable, it can be an act of selfishness to gain brownie points in the eyes of their peers and in the eyes of their God. I call this act – 'dirty giving'! True charity is 'clean' and comes from a place of gifting without needy wanting nor expecting something in return – a very rare occurrence in our paradigm. (More on the gift economy to come.)

The huwoman does not live in a world of morals based in duality, but lives and is comfortable in her own divinity, based on knowing that all is divine and connected. The huwoman does not live in a duality as a separating concept where good and evil and the lust of power and control exists. This is how we have acted for thousands of years and how we still reflect and worship God in his own image in our paradigm.

The huwoman's purpose is to live in the wonder of the gift of life itself, where the idea of worship does not exist but is replaced by words like respect, compassion, caring and trust in oneself.

Life is giving and loving towards everything in existence and not a dividing force created by God – to validate the CRAP system.

The huwoman lives in her own divinity, where division is not even a concept, because she lives in a fully operating trinity which is not divided and is all-encompassing. She is autonomous and yet connected to the whole. She does not have needs based on attachment, nor is she restricted by fear, but is in touch with her fear and uses it in a manner which gives her a sensible approach and healthy respect for life. She moves freely, connecting with all that surrounds her, untroubled by the past or the future. She lives fully in the moment.

After reading the paragraph above a friend asked, 'Is it possible to divide a trinity?'

My answer is – yes! Of course, one can divide a trinity – in this paradigm we do it all the time. However, when we divide a trinity we create separation. In that separation we get a duality and a singularity or three singularities all trying to connect to each other for stability, creating an existence filled with tension and instability in the trying. It is like removing one structural element of any structure – there is only so much propping up that can be done before it collapses. A healthy trinity is not divided, but connected to all its aspects, and all its aspects are in a balanced relationship with each other.

It is also commonly believed that we, as humans, are here to learn. To learn what?

I think a more accurate description is that we are here to experience the wonder of animated life. Animated life is created by the grace of biodiversity shaped by the organic technology that stems from the trinity of space, energy and matter – divinity itself.

We are made from, and of, that divinity. At death, our physicality is returned to matter then recycled. The part of us that lives on is energy, our awareness. This is what manifests matter, according to the imaginative ability which has been accumulated through organic evolutions from a biodiverse array of species.

Humanity seems to be in agreement that life is a struggle. We are a species built on out-of-control fear: fear of ourselves, fear of each other and fear of the power of our beautiful planet. The wars between each other are endless. Whether internally or globally, war is based on the fear of losing power and control. We war to control and oppress each other and to possess Gaia's resources by creating destruction and imbalance all around us.

Most of our respected institutions are based on the psychology of fear – our governments, our laws and religious institutions to name a few. Dig a little deeper and you will find that our culture is built and based on the fear of just about everything.

Fear is a friend and necessary for survival in that it warns us of danger and triggers appropriate action – it becomes a foe when it is the modus operandi – the legacy of the CRAP system. How do we not realise that we are warring not only with our planet, but with ourselves and our own species. Are we not all from the same species? Are we not all homo sapiens? Homo sapiens (ironically) means, wise human.

Is struggle part of the duality system of where we are either at war or at peace, and peaceful conflict resolution escapes us? Why should existence be a struggle? Existence isn't a struggle; we make it a struggle by the way we have disconnected from ourselves and our surroundings.

Can we exist without struggle in a huwoman evolution?

Personally, I think we can. In my experience as an artist, I create best with my imagination in a place that is free of struggle. It is in the experience of giving birth to my imagination where I feel discomfort as I travel through the birth canal of the possibilities of the imagination. I call this 'the pain of creation', different to the pain and suffering we cause each other for goodness knows what.

Yes, there is a lot of work to be done to create the huwoman. The pain of giving birth comes with any new life in its creation. I find solace in knowing that the growth, pain and sacrifice needed to create the huwoman will be our balance and future survival.

The fear and struggle to survive is primordial as we need food, water and shelter to survive. Surviving without struggle is to be at the helm of one's own creative destiny and accepting humbly what is in our every moment. The huwoman will look primordial and appreciate her sensory primordial-ness, however, she will not think nor act in the same primordial psychology of our present, nor deny her primordial her-it-age. Killing for food and for the pleasure of taking a life will not be part of her DNA.

I can hear a question coming from you – how do I re-main peaceful if someone is acting dangerously towards me? Acknowledge that this is your present situation and without falling into the panic of being a victim, use the energy of your fear to come to your senses and find the quickest and best way out of that situation. Basically, get yourself the hell out of there and deal with the emotional side effects later and in the appropriate moment.

If you don't make it out, then remember to hold on to your awareness while passing, not of that moment, but awareness of who you are outside your physical – divinity itself.

The huwoman is in touch with her divinity and the uni-versal heart which lives inside her. She has the ability to create from that imaginative heart filled with the stream of love consciousness rather than with the physically needy emotional love consciousness of our present un-derstanding of love. With and through that stream of love consciousness she will be engaged in the constant creation of peace, kindness and harmony.

I can hear another question coming. Who created the universal heart and where does it exist? Ha-ha!

The universal heart is a figure of speech describing the universe and the ultimate force of nature. It is the intelligence of the universe. It exists everywhere and it is omnipresent. It is inside and around us and in the space where we think there is nothing. We need awareness of its existence to tap into it – and the self-awareness to live in and with it in harmony.

Who created the universal heart? Well, that's the same as asking who created the universe? The universe is not created by a whom it is that which just is. It has evolved by its own force of nature and continues to evolve without a whom. Its building blocks cannot be created nor destroyed – why is it that so difficult to comprehend?

The universe is physical and ethereal at the same time. It is omnipresent, it surrounds everything and because it is a living breathing organism it is in constant self-creation. It is neither male or female because they are concepts of a duality paradigm and one of many possible paradigms. The possibilities depend on the imaginative capabilities of a species and we are one of them. If there were such a thing as a deity, the universe is our deity.

The universe is the force of nature and everything is made by the power of self-sustaining organic technology, constantly in self-creation. The universal heart is the spirit of the universe, just like matter is the physical and energy is the soul of the same.

The physical engine of the universe is matter, energy is the soul or the fuel, and the force of the universe – the universal heart – is the spirit; the intelligence of and the driving force which unites all the aspects of the universe for creation.

The body is the engine, the fuel is the soul and the spirit is the driver. The soul connects with the physical, the spirit connects to the physical through the soul, the spirit connects to the universe – the playground of the imagination. When one's soul is at peace, then one's images emanating from one's spirit will reflect that of one's soul core in the astral plane of ethereal light and in the world – that is how one recreates oneself – changing one's sound, images and psychology, to affect the physical and create a huwoman in a life of peace, in peace.

As the universal heart cannot be measured in a test tube or by an instrument, it is considered non-existent, to our own detriment. The universal heart is a stream of consciousness – it can only be known through personal experience which comes from inner knowing and is in the measure of oneself. To know, is in the realm of knowing. To be in the realm of knowledge is to know little and especially of the universal heart.

We can consciously live in the stream of the universal heart like the huwoman, or we can deny its existence and continue to work against it as we have done in our human condition, where lack of connection, lack of self-awareness and lack of the consequences of destructive and annihilating actions prevail. When imagination is thwarted, our fantasies based on fear take over and we continue to create in fear, based on our fantasies of reality.

Full awareness is knowing that physical life originated miraculously by the imaginative intelligence of one cell. All animated life came from the drive of that one cell to evolve. That cell worked out how it would divide over time to build our entire organism, made up of trillions of cells. That is pure imaginative intelligence, and we are made of that imaginative intelligence. The potential for our cells to find new and more sustainable ways to organically evolve is a real possibility only limited by our imagination as a species.

Full awareness is also knowing that the physical form is an illusion of many possibilities created by the level of our imaginative spirit, accumulated in each evolution. When the physical takes itself too seriously it develops an ego. Life then becomes a delusion, difficult to get out of, as it lacks imagination. Ego-based fantasy then becomes the reality of a culture standing on an edge of the precipice of a very precarious future.

In contrast, the huwoman comes from her imagination in the present moment reality, that is always linked to universal consciousness, not from some future or past notion of reality based on fantasy coloured by indoctrination, fear and often unconscious self-loathing. In the present moment she acts with imagination and trusts her observation via her senses, informing her to create appropriate action in any given moment – she does not operate from anger or from an attitude that she is owed anything. She is the giver. She is the receiver. She is the gift.

Imagination is creative manifestation in the true meaning of creation.
Pure imagination does no harm, unlike fantasy.

The huwoman physical body

At present, the huwoman's physical body is in a prototype stage and open to the many possibilities for evolution. However, I imagine that the huwoman looks physically primordial while at the same time losing our present primordial thinking for the need to hunt and gather to feed herself.

Skeletal

An approximate height of 1.8m will be the ideal. The skeleton will be similar to today's but with some adjustments and modifications, including stronger and larger knee joints to support and allow a cushioning effect and for strength in supporting the back and torso during movement. It will also be able to heal itself without the consequences of calcification and injury-based arthritis, and the limbs and organs will be replaceable by regeneration if needed. The abdominal area will be slightly larger and stronger to support cellular storage for energy and the legs will be somewhat longer, with larger feet for stability and balance. The whole skeletal structure will be strong yet flexible at the same time.

Body shape

The huwoman body will look similar to the modern-day human with a few modifications. The main part of the body will be a combination of a short, possibly green/khaki colour cashmere-type fur and a tough light absorbing skin for the chest, hands, feet, face and upper back for energy efficiency and improved absorption of light.

Her appearance will not be in line with our present notion of aesthetics and will be a combination of many of our world's human physical shapes. However, one must remember that aesthetics change depending on our environment, our culture and our dominant values. So, what looks beautiful to us now may not be practical and may be inappropriate in our new form. Our aesthetic for women, especially in the media today, is to look physically small, disabled by inappropriate shoes and skimpily dressed to present as a sexual object for man's pleasure. I personally don't find any of this aesthetically pleasing and yet many do because these are the images presented for survival, especially as a woman living in the CRAP system. We live in an obtuse system lead by men which renders women stupid enough to follow their obtusity.

High heels keep women restricted, unnecessarily keeps them on their toes and unnecessarily creates bodily damage.

The non-genital huwoman takes pleasure through her heightened sensory perceptions and is genital-less because she does not need to remove waste from food or procreate with them – she has no need for genitals. I find it interesting that we have been hearing a lot about gender these days and wonder if in our clumsy obtusity we are preparing for the huwoman already? There is big business in gender genital rearrangement.

Maybe if we didn't have to poo and piss, we wouldn't be in the psychology of needing to piss and poop everywhere and on everything – even in that respect, the huwoman is considerate.

If women and men don't wake up and create the huwoman's psychology within to save ourselves, then it is inevitable that the male psychology of survival will kill us all and women will tag along.

Reproduction

In relation to procreation, the huwoman will reproduce herself once in a lifespan through a 'testrogen' (huwoman word), a hormonal impulse that produces a self-fertilising small embryo-type foetus which will develop in a pouch-like structure (much like a kangaroo) carried where the abdominal area now exists. As the huwoman will need light energy storage in the abdominal area, it makes sense to have an incubator outside and part of the dermis. The fertilised egg will be produced internally and without the need of another as she has both sexes within her. This non-cloning and non-parthenogenesis being, will have the ability to produce testrogen that comes from both her combined female and male aspects of her biology.

The reproductive system has a failsafe switch – so to speak – so that if necessary, the embryo can be retarded and kept alive in status until such time as the conditions are right. If there are problems in the foetal stages of development, it can be kept in status until it is healed or replaced without encumbrance to the parent. In the case where an adult for some reason has died before giving birth then the communities' deep connectedness to each other will trigger a second child in others, while still keeping the population small and sustainable.

Offspring

The offspring will retain all the memories and experiences of the parent and ancestral past, giving her the ability to start from a place of awareness and knowing without having to reinvent the wheel each time. Imagine not having to go through the paradox and the attitude of the teenage years thinking you know everything, when you know very little.

In our present paradigm each generation has to learn the gained knowledge and wisdom of its ancestors from scratch and in our present paradigm each generation is influenced by the ego-based perspective of the present governing system being capitalism, religion and patriarchy – the CRAP system – where wisdom is not encouraged and the young are exploited for monetary gain.

We are an intelligent species, there is no doubt about that, however, intelligence without wisdom is not intelligent but stupidity and becomes destructive. Coupled with the governing CRAP system of our present paradigm, it is leading us to eventual annihilation. If we are born knowing, then we have wisdom, and as wisdom is learnt and earned, the huwoman child with her accumulated wisdom from her ancestors will be in a position to contribute wisely and with respect from a nonviolent perspective.

I can hear you saying – and you may well ask – what about the pleasure of physical touch with another? Sharing physical experiences with another will be for companionship and the experience of pleasure, rather than from a hormonal sense of desperate release for procreation. Like all the other senses developed in this evolution, touch, and to be touched, will be from an experience of sensual bliss in a way that few of us can understand.

Pleasure from the senses is sensual rather than sexual and not performance based. The huwoman is fully sensual and in the pleasure of the fullness of her sensory awareness of life. To be fully in one's senses is to be omnipresent.

The offspring is taught and nurtured by the community until she is of age, which will depend on the lifespan of this species. The jury is still out on what the length of that lifespan may be – possibly a couple of hundred years with the offspring emerging around one third of the way through her lifespan. The huwoman will not age in the same way as the human; she will mature retaining her physical strength and flexibility. Her organic shape will transition around about the end of her lifespan surrounded by her community.

As part of their upbringing, children will be taught the importance that each individual makes to sustain a community. For example, the values of community living and being part of a caring, supportive, well-functioning, respectful and compassionate community where kindness prevails. They will also understand and know their environment and all other species it supports as part of their community – nothing is separate, all is connected, to make it whole. Unlike the present system of all for one and who cares if there is nothing left for anyone else.

Moisture and evaporation
When not needed to keep the mouth moist, beads of sweat evaporate through the skin.

Heart and circulation
The heart is modified to be connected to the energy storage area for the distribution and circulation of energy throughout the body.

Respiratory system

This species has the ability to inhale air and breathe in water for short periods of time. The lungs have a dual function of processing air through water with the aid of a small gill system behind her ears. The huwoman breathes air through the nose as normal.

Nervous system

Is not dissimilar than today, only modified for a larger variation of impulse sensitivity.

Muscular

Not dissimilar to today, only powered by natural light energy and whatever modifications needed for the variations in energy use.

Dermis

The dermis is light-penetrating and absorbing, holds warmth and is water resistant. The thin cashmere layer regulates insulation and protection from accidental damage, covering the back of the head, legs, arms, lower back and abdominal area including the pouch. The face, hands, feet, chest and upper back are covered in a tough light-absorbing skin for better and more efficient absorption of light energy. As well as absorbing storage light in the abdominal area for low light use, the dermis has its own storage system in a fat-like cellular structure substance sitting just beneath the skin for day use and quick bursts of energy. The skin will repair itself and leave no scarring – scarring will reduce light absorption capabilities.

Brain

The brain is large with one sphere and will do what our brain function does now, only it is fully accessible, having evolved to process information from the senses with high efficiency and sensitivity. It is also a receptor for intuitive and galactic information.

Head

Will consist of a large one hemisphere brain which is fully integrated and fully functioning, highly sensitive to stimuli from the senses including the sixth and a high sense of telepathy.

The face is similar to ours, the top and back of the head is covered with a cashmere coat (as mentioned) for protection. The brow is more defined to protect the eyes, which are dual functioning for day sight and night sight. Her eyes offer three sights: the sight with open eyes, the sight behind closed eyes and the sight during sleep.

Think how much time we spend with our eyes closed – yet we deny the life we have in that time and we see it as something not to be taken seriously, just part of the brain function. It is just as well we're not that conscious when it's happening, because that world does not adhere to the world of the eyes open. Whereas the huwoman lives in, is conscious of, and is able to integrate all three sights at the same time.

The nose is a little larger than today, for optimal breathing and is highly sensitive to scent. The pleasure of smell will be food for the soul. Hearing will also be exceptionally acute – in fact, all the senses will be highly evolved and highly sensitive to stimuli for survival and pleasurable experiences. With these highly developed senses, feelings of bliss form a natural daily occurrence.

The mouth contains a tongue and teeth necessary for language, sound and song. All that is necessary for sound in our present evolution will remain as is. Even though the huwoman does not need to eat, teeth remain, as they are important for speech. The huwoman teeth are strong in structure, permanent and solid – teeth can also double up as a tool if necessary.

Energy
This evolution of huwoman has the ability to absorb light through the skin and store it for energy, in a thin layer of fat-like substance beneath the skin for day movement, and within what is now the existing human digestive system for night or low light movement. The huwoman has a strong connection to her environment

and due to her adaptable functions is able to survive in a range of conditions.

The senses

The huwoman has highly developed senses, including her sixth sense which will awaken the ability for telepathy as another form of communication. The sense of taste will no longer be necessary and replaced by an awareness of sensibility uniting all senses for optimal pleasure and full presence for harmonious survival. After all, taste is there for the survival of a species powered by eating. It is there mainly for safety, for example, if you put something in your mouth and it taste horrible you will immediately spit out and avoid making yourself sick.

As well as not necessary in this evolution, the sense of taste could make us predatory again. When we remove taste this would enhance the other senses leaving us with smell, touch, sound, sight and telepathy to navigate our world. There is nothing more pleasurable than the senses when they are operating at their optimum efficiency. In our present culture our senses are dulled and we tend to unwittingly use our idea of something or fantasies to fill in the gaps and compensate for our lack of sense.

It never ceases to astound me how often I notice people see and hear what they want to see and hear and miss what is right in front of them because it does not fit in with their reality. Is it self-imposed blindness? Mostly, our senses are perceived through our belief system rather than reality based; we see and hear what we believe rather than what is really there.

To be fully in one's senses is to be in full awareness of one's surroundings, placing one's experience of life in the realm of omnipresent.

Defence system

As the peaceful huwoman species is non-predatory and nonviolent, does she need a defence system?

Defence unpacked
De-fence = taking away barriers
De-fence-less = having no barriers
De-fence-iveness = having barriers

Concepts of good and evil

To answer the question of whether a defence system is needed we need to explore good and evil. Does evil exist outside the conceptual physical world we create? Are good or evil concepts and if evil is conceptual is it possible for it to exist outside the physical? At this stage I have some awareness but no definite answer to that question. Just to be on the safe side, if I were to give her a defence system, the huwoman would need a peaceful pro-life mechanism in the form of camouflage, or shapeshifting abilities (there are already a number of animals with this ability) to be able to remove herself from the way of harm.

Those who control us also put us in the way of harm every day, making us lose trust in ourselves and each other and coercing us to find faith in our controllers and what they have to offer which is always with the view of the economics of capitalism – a patriarchal economy, reliant on destroying organic biodiversity for its survival.

Now that is pure evil!

There can be no dispute that this is the ultimate in evil because they have convinced us to go along with their obtuse plan to profit at any cost, even at the cost of life itself.

Evil does not seem to exist in the natural world and is therefore not part of organic technology. Evil appears to born of ego and of loss of power and control. Evil is conceptual and manifests in the physical experience of being human. This is what happens when we become disconnected from our minds (more on the mind to come) and from the Earth itself.

Thought without the aid of the mind and senses operates in fantasies devised from purely physical needs which in turn creates good and evil.

Evil is a manifestation of the physical which is usually enacted by those who are so fearful that they need to control and be in control to feel powerful. Due to being in ego-mode the physical is flawed with insecurities about itself, creating fear and mistrust and leading us to the dis-empowering loss of trust in ourselves, making us reliant to find faith in a system or some deity for reassurance and protection.

When good nor evil exist, we think and act in kindness. Kindness is kindred and kindred is connecting, and that is the psychology of a paradigm without the duality of good and evil. This is the paradigm within which the huwoman operates.

Trust and faith

The huwoman instinctively understands and trusts in her connection with all that exists rather than in our present systems of disbelief of anything other than the measurable physicality of matter. She also has the ability to understand, connect and communicate with the non-physical existing around her.

All matter is physical, the only difference is some matter is animate and some matter is inanimate — animate matter has a spark which makes it move. Keeping in mind that the original blueprint of the animate is originally created from imagination rather than fantasy. Creative imagination is the spark which motivates the animate and creates the inanimate. Imagination (unlike fantasy) is not conflicted but connected and considerate of all and to all, animate and inanimate.

Animals, like humans, are curious, but suspicious at the same time. They are ready to protect themselves in a fight, flight or freeze reaction. Trust is very slow to achieve. In contrast, the huwoman operates from knowing that trust is an action and mistrust is a reaction.

Trust, which comes from knowing, is different than faith. Faith is blind and blind faith is being a follower, giving away one's power, taking no responsibility and blaming others or the system when things don't quite go to plan.

To trust is not blind and is based on trust in oneself. Trust in oneself is knowing that in each given moment one will act appropriately, with considerate action and with humble respect for that moment. In trust, one is acting imaginatively rather than fearfully. Trust in oneself is being responsive and responsible towards our surroundings, knowing any action taken is not a reaction but is action taken from knowing. In this way, there is no need for fear of not trusting outside of oneself, because trust in oneself is what creates appropriate action towards that which surrounds us.

One is never responsible for another's actions, but always responsible for one's own actions. Acting from a place of kindness is disarming and promotes good will. In our present culture, we put ourselves in the way of harm every day, then we lose trust and we turn to faith.
Trust is knowing oneself. To trust in oneself is knowing you will be prepared to act in a caring manner with life situations as they arise. When you truly trust in yourself then trust is no longer an issue and there is no need to trust or mistrust anyone else.

Faith is giving up to the point of relinquishing control of one's life and allowing control of one's life by someone else and that someone else will give you salvation.

It takes courage to trust in oneself and weakness to put ourself in the way of faith.

The evil of the CRAP system is on a non-stoppable trajectory to the point of it being the norm, going unnoticed in our culture, so much so that we have become the cogs of its machine to stay alive. We have lost trust in our inner knowing and have converted it into faith – faith that we are in good hands and that the CRAP system will look after us. Evil only looks after itself!

Our present trajectory, orchestrated by the CRAP system, is not going to be able to get itself out of its primordial mess as it continues to use the same solution over and over, for the problems it creates, while expecting change.

'Insanity is doing the same thing over and over and expecting different results.'

Albert Einstein

The CRAP system will keep chasing its fantasised tail with more and more solutions out of desperation by tampering with nature, until there is no more to tamper with. This is the present human's destructive psychology in the guise of progress that has invaded the Earth space, the astral space and our psychology.

We live in a world where social contagion is everywhere and is (of course) encouraged by the CRAP system. Imagine if we were all truly integrated in wisdom within ourselves and we did not need the validation of mass

contagion to govern us, and in the process, fooling ourselves into believing we must be right if everyone else
thinks the same.

Good and evil do not exist in a trinity, they are based in dualism.
In a trinity there is peace, kindness and respect in balance.

PART TWO

IMAGINATION LOST: THE CONSEQUENCES OF OUR FANTASIES

Thought and thought imagery emit energy in electromagnetic waves. These electromagnetic waves are energy in motion. Depending on the clarity and intensity of the thought and or image they will travel and therefore, continue to exist outside of ourselves. Often these ethereal thoughts and thought images hover around us, affecting the energy space of what is commonly known as the astral, which lives just at the edge of our consciousness.

The awareness of the astral by humans is rare and therefore in the realm of disbelief and outside the plane of fabricated knowledge. However, believe it or not, when I venture into the astral, I see a lot of ethereal imagery and more often patriarchal imagery. It is quite likely that when we die, we as consciousness also hover in our thought imagery in the astral plane as energy entwined in images.

Currently, in my experience, the astral is full of ethereal imagery that portrays our fantasies and delusions. Only when we change the astral, consciously and with intent, to create with positive imagination can the new future begin to emerge. Because what we place in the astral with our thoughts and corresponding actions are the reflective tools of evolution we have to work with.

It is not possible to create beyond our fantasies if we can't imagine, so start imaging with new and positive images which transform our actions towards ourselves and our environment. To do so now is critical to our future survival.

The astral plane houses our subconscious (the bit of us that follows), unconscious (what we do without realising) and conscious (the bit that gives direction). While there, and especially after physical death, we recreate ourselves from the tools we have projected throughout our lives through our thoughts, images and actions into the ethereal astral plane. When we create ourselves subconsciously, we create ourselves from a limited awareness and with the thought imagery we have accepted as our reality – and in a perpetuating belief system where we see ourselves belonging to specific family groups. We act from this delusion into an illusion which is projected on Earth; it can never end until we create anew. Is this potentially where the notion of reincarnation and family ties comes from? The astral plane is like a movie screen of our present fantasised life in perpetual creation from a primordial awareness of flight, freeze or fight psychology.

If one can move through the astral at physical death without entanglement, but with awareness, then liberation from our present entanglement becomes possible. At this stage, the possibilities to create new illusions where energy and matter are harmoniously connected becomes possible. Whereas, in our present paradigm, our belief system suppresses the awareness of truly creative imagination and the possibilities to create beyond the present astral plane of fantasy imagery with organic technology.

To pass beyond the present astral plane to create anew one must retain a level of awareness, one must know and recognise the stream of love consciousness and move with it, and one must not stay caught up in the emotional and binding attachment consciousness mistaken for love.

If we remain in the illusionary plane of the astral without awareness, we just get recycled into the genetics of our ties and entanglements of the present paradigm and with no awareness that we have the ability for change with endless possibilities. This keeps us trapped in the present paradigm of our fantasies. Like in our nightly dream state, in our astral state we don't generally remember our time there, which makes it difficult to understand, let alone prove. And of course, the patriarchal paradigm places science between the astral and ourselves, because according to them, nothing exists unless it can be measured, tagged and mutilated, to delude themselves and those who have an inkling that there is more to life and death. To compensate we are given religion as a substitute which replaces our deep inner knowing with ideology that supports the patriarchy and subscribes to fabricated knowledge, dogma and violence in its name.

This is also how the collective unconscious works, where most are born unconsciously bringing their ancestral delusions with them. Just as we prepare and hone our skills for life, work and play, we must also prepare for the journey after physical death. Isn't it time we stop faithfully complying with the CRAP system which is in the process of self-imploding? To not do otherwise, is to continue to support it by acting in the same game we have played for centuries which is getting us closer to... need I spell it out? Surely you would opt for action in peaceful alignment with nature, of which we are a part of. Are we so dead inside that we have lost our humanity and our will to live altogether?

Let's learn to pass with awareness that all is possible, so change can be orchestrated in the non-physical realm as well. I wonder if with awareness at death one can choose not to be reborn as an act of humanity. Are we all born with a driving consciousness or are some born as purely a physical entity without an inner driving consciousness? To imagine and create a new physical illusion based on positive images of the huwoman, once our physical dies, we must hang on to our awareness of imagination rather than our fantasy of thought and create ourselves anew without images of the CRAP system. The impetuous to create comes from universal consciousness energy, which needs sensory perception to experience the joy of pleasure only animated physicality can give.

Energy works through and with light and we are energy alight, shaped into matter. The same as in the physical realm, humans create objects by shaping matter according to their skillset and creative abilities. Universal energy also creates according to the awareness of our imagination, gathered from physicality. Until energy and matter can be organised into a harmonious illusion, we remain stagnant and stuck in a paradigm of our making. Most of us do not know how to change our present predicament because we are so entrenched in the illusion of this reality. Remember, unless we change this illusion of our reality we are heading for extinction, or at the very least, unthinkable suffering. I am not sure we realise the enormous ramifications and implications of our actions, not only for the planet, but also for universal evolvement. It has taken an unthinkable amount of time for energy, matter and the chemistry of organic biodiversity to shape the evolutions of the present species living on Earth – let's not completely destroy it with our carelessness.

Every species on Earth, that is, anything shaped from matter in the universe, is shaped according to the intelligence and degree of ability by that species to evolve for better survival in the physical. I call this innate need for physical survival the imaginative intelligence of species, which in other words, is the awareness of mind imagination and that intelligence is in every cell of every organic living animate and inanimate thing. We are shaped from the same imaginative intelligence of matter substance! Only in this paradigm do we believe that the inanimate is dead and we are alive.

Everything in nature is animated in its own way – just like us the animate, the inanimate is always in the process of change and restructuring itself, only it does not have the superiority issues of the animate human. All nature must be respected and not taken for granted.

Actors in the universal stage

What fools we are! As humans we don't 'mind think' we 'brain think' and this is our problem. We think that intelligence is having a large brain and since we have a large brain, and we are top of the food chain, we are more evolved and therefore more important. We also believe that as a species god gave us this planet to do with as we wish – and we therefore have the right to do as we wish with other species as well, with the arrogance of taking no responsibility for the consequence of our actions. We are the gods of death or should I say the Dogs of Death.

Being at the top of the food chain is a privilege and privilege comes with responsibilities to look after those born lower on the food chain. Every animate and inanimate object has a role in sustaining and maintaining the health and longevity of our home planet. In reality we are superfluous to this planet and act with such misguided arrogance to the detriment of all.

It's not the size of the brain, but the way it's wired, which creates intelligence and wisdom.

Unlike most animals, who are both food for each other and feed on each other, while humans can be eaten, they are really not on anyone's menu. Yet as a species, just about everything is on our menu and we are ferocious eaters without limits. Not only that but we are also extravagantly wasteful. Wasting food is sacrilege! And we in the west do it every day!!

As a species our planet does not need us for its survival but we do need our planet for ours – it is as simple as that. Still, it seems to go over most people's heads. A species with that much privilege has responsibilities towards the preservation of the planet and yet it has its hand constantly in Mother Nature's till – planet slaughter and genocide have no greater rival as the ultimate crime and we are all guilty in this respect and sentencing ourselves to death.

The consequences of what we do on the universal stage is that we diminish the universe by removing the actors made from the already established building blocks of matter, over thousands of years, leaving energy, light and matter adrift while aimlessly waiting for some impetus like an asteroid collision to regroup.

When all those building blocks of organised animated matter disintegrate, the accumulated intelligence of the universe is adrift and having to start the long process of creating animated life again to rehouse that accumulated intelligence. Without the already established building blocks in existence, this could severely thwart the conscious awareness and imaginative intelligence of the universe itself.

This is where my urgency comes from; we are perilously on the brink of no return but continue as if it's not happening.

I don't know about you but I notice that at present the growing human psychology is, 'Who cares if we live or die as a species – we are so despicable.' Yes, as a species we do despicable things to ourselves and to others, however, we have evolved into an amazingly beautiful structure. We have the ability to be conceptual and our physical bodies have evolved to be able to actualise our conceptualness like no other animal can – we are impressive! Not only are we amazing but we are so close to evolving into a physical entity (the huwoman) who can fully encompass that which exists outside the physical realm as well. Why destroy ourselves when the next evolution can, and will be, that of the huwoman who is fully realised?

People, we are so close to magnificence. We already have the building blocks. Let's build on them, rather than destroy them.

It is imperative that we start imaging the sustainable huwoman evolution by using our already established building blocks to take us further into the necessary evolution needed for our physical existence. Aborting our building blocks now and heading for premature extinction is of great loss to the universal consciousness.

When a species becomes prematurely extinct, they have not had the opportunity of time for their imaginative intelligence to adjust to a sustainable evolution, which then becomes lost from the universe forever. However, when natural extinction happens, it is not lost but absorbed, a necessary process for universal evolution. Forced mass extinction, on the other hand, has no due process and all is lost because energy becomes imagine-less without its actors. What we are creating is a similar situation to a massive accident of some sort where many prematurely die, leaving irreparable loss and devastation.

Atomic energy

Everything material is made of atoms – one could say everything is atomic intelligence! What happens when we play with the fundamental building blocks of matter? Are we playing Russian roulette with the fundamental building blocks of the universe? Although matter and energy cannot be destroyed, when we split the atom, we convert matter into energy. We then become victims of this madness – our planet and all that belong to her are affected by having to absorb added radiation that we are not equipped to deal with. There are far too many problems to mention in this small book, but each adds incrementally to the health problems of every living creature – just look at the rise in cancer alone.

Since 1945 there have been over 2000 nuclear detonations. Slowly but surely these nuclear detonations are creating and adding to the colossal and devastating human induced climate change – and what for? Because men like to play with crackers? And to justify their actions, they tell us it is in the aid of progress for humanity. Again, what for? To produce energy for a population we cannot sustain anyway? To go to Mars? To destroy each other with nuclear weapons?

In biological systems, matter and energy are never converted from one to the other, there is always the same amount of matter and energy. Therefore, neither is created, destroyed or used like the modern physicist does to play god by creating a physi-cist (physical cyst) in the fabric of our world.

Energy needed to eat

Eating makes us primordial and in this paradigm our primordial-ness is ruled and dominated by patriarchal values that adopt capitalism and religion as a way of thinking for power and control. Our actions stem from that basic need for food to survive and, to satisfy our essential needs, we not only kill to eat but we kill for pleasure. Consider, if having enough to eat is our main motivation, what motivates anyone who does not need to eat or kill?

In our paradigm, because we are ruled by warlords, these basic needs turn into greed and lust and an insatiable thirst to conquer and destroy, wasting precious resources for personal gain. Ultimately, we war with each other, stealing each other's territories and pretending our actions are about protecting ourselves in self-defence and for misguided patriotism. These actions amount to male primordial-ness with the need to provide and compete like bulls, seek dominance and acquire spoils for themselves and all for their glorification so that they will attract a woman. In this world even women can become prey so that they can be 'preyed' upon if not compliant. Is this not the unconscious manifestation of the lust for dominance and of the hunt so man can prove his seed for procreation is the best?

And women readily comply because they too are blinded by the delusion of the patriarchal trinity operating from a duality! What's worse is that women and men believe this is it, that there is no other possibility than our present trajectory and there is nothing we can do to course correct.

Let's leave our primordial 'mess' behind by creating survival from awareness, where we use the power of the imaginative mind as a vehicle for expansiveness coming from companionate consciousness, which contributes to universal intelligence. Rather than from the primordial annihilating and subtraction method that operates in our twenty-first century paradigm. The primordial psychology of us is thinking that expansion is a forward trajectory, and with the tools and weapons we have built to secure our primordial future along with our primordial fantasies, makes us very dangerous indeed, not only to ourselves and each other, but also for anything which is in our way. We destroy environments and people like swatting flies.

Expansion and continuous progress from our primordial psychological perspective becomes, over time, retractionist, reductionist and implosive to the point of extinction.

Artificial sound

To aid us in our summoning of the huwoman transition within, we must reduce our sounds from inharmonious to harmonious with nature, our natural home. We make, especially by the male aspect of our duality, a lot of noise in the artificial world we have created.

There is a lot of noise: machinery, cars, wars, anger, pain, the endless noise from the mowing of lawns and on and on it goes – all inharmonious with our natural surroundings. Natural sounds are calming and flow. Machinery sounds overpower and jar. As sound travels, we are deafening the natural world and ourselves with all our noise!

Because we need air to breath for life and have senses to keep us alive, we can make sound and hear it; this is because sound needs the same air that we breathe. Sound is vibrating air, and travels in air. What a privilege! Let's reconnect with the natural sounds of nature and of our planet and make less artificial sounds by slowing down the cogs of the CRAP system. This can only be done by reducing our population to a sustainable number as an act of self-preservation. You'll find my population solution in my previous book, *Questions from a Sometimes Philosopher Looking For Utopia*.

The sound of our language becomes the way we move. Change the sounds of your language to change the energy you move with. Change your energy with the sounds you make and the words you use.

When our language is aggressive, then we physically want to be aggressive. All the swear words are aggressive – how do you feel when someone swears at you?

When our language is peaceful, we feel peaceful and we want to be kind. Words like kindness, connection, beautiful – how do they make you feel?

Swear words bring up fight and (if sensible) flight. Kind words do neither. They make you feel like staying. Staying in kindness is a third and balanced option. This doesn't mean a repressed anger. It means that with kindness, there is less need for anger, and when there is unbalance, one can work through that in the kindest possible way.

The sign of a disintegrating culture is when the language of that culture is substituted with the language of swearing. A culture with a diminished language lacks depth of understanding and the experience of life is restricted – language like imagination is evolutionary. Interestingly, the biggest insult in our culture one can make is the one that refers to a woman's genitalia – wow, if that's not deep rooted in our internalised misogyny.

∞

As humans, anger is part of our emotional and psychological release mechanism and is at times unavoidable. However, anger is also energy and can be used destructively towards ourselves and others, or it can be used creatively with integrity, thoughtful compassionate action and with respect for not only ourselves and those around us, but also towards our planet. With conscious awareness, anger can be positively channelled in so many creative and simple ways, for example, going for a walk, putting it in writing, taking positive action, gardening … the list is endless. One must find one's own creative and positive way in releasing anger without being hurtful, because ultimately we have found ourselves in our present position by our previous actions and blame is not helpful. Past present and future are connected and intertwined.

By living in the awareness of our actions and their consequences we become empowered to create our lives in a meaningful way rather than becoming a victim of our own anger. The huwoman is not in a language of anger but is in a language of peace. Peace is what unites love or hate and brings love or hate into a peaceful trinity.

Come on people, let's get it together. We are capable. How can we address what needs to be done if we're sleepwalking in a delusion created for us to participate in the CRAP scheme, free of charge, and with our life. Those of us who live in a so-called dwindling democracy are the biggest abusers of the natural world and yet have the power to change that. Not by just lip service, but by taking action in our everyday lives with the things we do, use and create. And yet we don't; or it's not fast enough to make a real difference.

Artificial light

The only light which is not artificial is that of sunlight, moonlight and starlight (another trinity) and that light is from the life-giving source of organics used by plants to grow and for animals to navigate and so much more. Artificial light is all around us giving humans night sight to keep us safe – supposedly.

Artificial light pollutes our sky, so much so that we can no longer see nor connect clearly with the wonders of the stars of our universe. Artificial light is visual noise and confuses our sensory perception of the world around us. It's not enough that we do this to ourselves but our artificial light affects all the flora and fauna of our organic world which relies on the three natural sources of light to navigate life. Again, you may say, 'Poppycock!' – I say, do the research yourself. We are so disconnected from our natural environment that we can no longer see or feel the effects of our pollution with our short-term vision.

The huwoman has developed night vision in addition to day vision, making her able to live harmoniously with her natural environment. Let's start needing less artificial light to navigate our world, allowing nature to do its work of the dark. Using less artificial light is also beneficial in reducing global warming as it adds excess heat into the air. In fact, anything we do to preserve our planet in our daily lives is an act of spirituality. Spirituality is of the essence of the Earth and the universe.

I regularly do the exercise outlined below – you may wish to try it if you feel safe doing so.

In the early mornings and evenings, I often walk around the house pottering around in natural light. Once my eyes become adjusted to the soft light, I am always surprised how much natural light comes through windows and when the moon is full and bright the house becomes illuminated with the power of the moon. This exercise helps to hone in on and strengthen the senses. It trains my eyesight to be less reliant on artificial light and it saves energy as I am using most of my sensory perceptions to navigate around my house. My thoughts then also become a tool for my senses rather than my ego. Ask an eye sightless person how they navigate the world without artificial light. Actually, without any light.

Oh, yes, it may bring up fear, but remember that fear is having a healthy respect for life. If not reacted upon, but acted upon by moving with it and through it with aware-ness, then fear becomes your friend – doing what it does best, helping you to navigate the world in a sensible manner.

You can do these sorts of exercises with all your senses – for example, spend a day in awareness of your hearing, reminding yourself to listen to the sounds around you and observe how the different sounds affect you.

Another practice is to switch off your internet at night. Such a very simple thing everyone can do at the press of a button. This small action will make a huge difference to the planet's carbon footprint. It's not that difficult: press the on/off button at the back of your modem as an act of conscious awareness towards our planet and ourselves. This is an act of true spirituality because spirituality is about awareness of one's connectedness to everything and everything you do in kindness for the planet you do for you as well. Imagine if everyone in Australia did this simple action every evening before going to bed – wow! What an impact we would make.

Progress in the lack of sanity

Our ability to be conceptual is in conflict with our primordial needs creating artificiality as a screen between the two and disconnecting us from ourselves and our surroundings. The sustainable huwoman's primordial need is to expand the mind, the possibilities of which are life-giving, endless and causative.

In our current paradigm we seem to be in a hurry for so called progress – for what? Our scientific and technological advancement makes us falsely believe that our ongoing survival is in good hands. However, all we are doing is reacting and creating with primordial consciousness, heading with great velocity to our premature extinction. If we start to slow down, reduce our population and truly reflect on our trajectory, it will become obvious that we have lost our sanity.

Consider 'insane', a word to describe a person who has gone mad. However, to be in sanity means to be sane or dwell in sanity. 'Out-sane' or out of sanity is what we have become. We are disrespecting and interfering with the natural technology of the biosphere by destroying it and not allowing the process of time for the biosphere to regenerate and use its amazing inbuilt organic technology, to shape and mould for the long game of survival, in a manner for life-giving longevity of the planet and the species who inhabit our planet.

Look how magnificently far the biosphere's natural technology has got us and with no help or interference from science technology. We have inherited and live in the most exquisitely biodiverse planet known, and we are now not only tampering with it but destroying it with technology which comes from capitalist ego-based science. We see this as expansion but it is reductionist to the point of no return. Technological science based on capitalism is delusional in thinking that it can compete, surpass and create life or replace organic life, originally created by organic biosphere technology. Our planet is organic, therefore, it is more malleable and open to change than we realise or believe, because our beliefs are fabricated and imposed on us by the CRAP system.

If we want to use science technology as an aid or tool, it needs to be sustainable and in harmony with our surrounding biosphere. It must also be reined in and remain within the realms of a tool rather than a copier of, usurper of and destroyer of organic life.

Organics and artificiality don't mix because artificiality is at the expense of organics, using its properties to make substances which it cannot absorb. The organic world then becomes a suffocated storage facility for inorganics.

Organic architecture is another area we are all drawn to – built over billions of years, the wonders of organic planning and design. We build our homes by deconstructing that organic architecture and then pollute it with inorganics, and we do this carelessly and mindlessly. We keep growing in the name of progress like a virus and unless we put an end to it we are perpetuating the same destructive cycle over and over until there is nothing left to progress and expand into to. The paradox of duality and the consequences when that paradox is governed by the CRAP system is the system of death.

Technological science is a paradox; it appears to open our eyes but in actual fact it blinds and thwarts our senses rendering us to become dependent on a system which is not in our best interest for survival. Are the alarm bells ringing?

We have created so much dead inorganic material with the pillaging of our organic world and continually replace our natural environment and ourselves with it. What folly! Are we so stupid as to not appreciate what and where we are? What kind of obtuse system will replace itself and its surroundings with dead stuff, annihilating itself just for the illusion of power and money to become inorganic? Our future biology is rapidly being replaced by inorganic technology, meaning we will communicate with inorganic entities and in the process, replace ourselves to be able to do so. What the …!

Inorganic is anti-life. Organic is life itself, is alive and in touch with knowing when organic evolution is necessary. To aid organic technology that evolves us into a much-needed sustainable huwoman, it is necessary to start imagining and acting towards our evolution, not from fantasy but from the imagination that goes beyond knowledge and towards knowing. Knowing that our trajectory is way off course and knowing that it is time to take a step back to reflect and act for the survival of organic life, is a good start to knowing. To put it simply technology is killing the very thing it and we need to survive – the Earth.

Organic technology and 'organic-transmitters'

When we watch a flock of birds or even a school of fish we notice they appear to swim, fly and forage quite happily, seemingly unconnected to each other. If a trigger of some sort happens, the whole school or flock instinctively organise themselves to join and become one. The intelligence of 'organic-transmitters' is all around us and every species on earth is connected to it. Interestingly, this is a reflection of the inner workings of the atoms in every living cell and how they instinctively organise themselves to create a mass.

We are the only creatures who are disconnected from each other and our surrounds, all the while trying to find our connection through artificial nonorganic means. It's as if we despise ourselves so much that we have lost touch with who we truly are. Not only do we no longer appreciate who we are and what we have, we seem intent on replacing ourselves with artificial technology – it's like we are trying to amputate and replace a damaged limb, only it is us we are amputating and all for the benefit of the 'powerfools' who control to create from their fantasies and in an unconscious and desperate effort to give birth in their own image. Let's cease to continue to support the dogs who think they are gods.

That, to me, is the definition of suicide by lack of sanity. When we can no longer appreciate who we are and what we have, everything becomes pointless other than self-destruction with the power for complete annihilation.

As Albert Einstein said:

'Imagination is the highest form of research.'

'We cannot solve our problems with the same thinking we used when we created them.'

'The world as we have created it is a process of our think-ing. It cannot be changed without changing our thinking. If the facts don't fit the theory, change the facts.'

∞

Be in awareness of imaginative thought rather than in the fantasies of thought to create a peaceful future.

The inner war against organic technology and the shadow

The war began the moment we started wearing shoes! Wearing shoes to protect our feet meant that we no longer needed to watch our step carefully. We could now more carelessly and thoughtlessly stomp on the seemingly invisible organic life on the ground beneath us.

Thus, creating a disconnecting layer between us, the earth and our primordial-ness. Ever since we have been conflicted within and at war with our biodiversity, its organisms and all that is part of organic technology. In other words, we stopped treading lightly and respectfully. Try walking in nature in bare feet and you will see what I mean.

This inner conflict is reflected in the psychology of our present patriarchal system of control. It is a belief system based on power and the need to control in the delusional thinking that it can outsmart organic technology with its own technology. In this egoic system, wars are created and justified by making them someone else's fault and that it is an act in self-defence. They claim we are at war with China or Russia or whoever they can create a money-making enemy out of, at any given time. This is how this system deals with its inner conflict with its organic nature and unconsciously reflects it outwards. And it is in this perilous system we place our faith for a future.

The shadow is an unconscious aspect of a personality or society driven by primal instinct, projected out, usually without awareness and often conflicting.

There are three main shadows woven into our underlying psychology looming over our existence.

Our first projected shadow is that we perceive our primordial-ness as primitive and uneducated therefore unscientific, barbaric and war-like, unintelligent, unknowledgeable, stagnant and lacking in wisdom. This mistaken belief makes us uncomfortable and unwilling to admit that primordial is our very inner core and the underlying psychology it carries.

It is this false unconscious self-loathing psychology which creates the shadow we cast upon our actions which in turn creates the barbaric, war-like, unintelligent, unwise and self-destructive paradigm we have created and are still creating and enacting.

It may be said by some that the following is a myth, even so, the fact that this myth exists shows the psychology in Australia, especially by the first invaders, who considered the original inhabitants – who were in the fullness of their primordial-ness – as fauna. An excuse to de-humanise and demonise them so that with all good and godly conscious intentions the powers that be could jus-tifiably remove them and cut them down like a forest without remorse. After all, they were just part of the flora and fauna and the god of the colonialists gave man au-thority over flora and fauna!

The result of 2023 referendum in Australia showed that the attitudes from 200 or so years have not changed and have been carried over to the present.

To the Aboriginal people of this land, thank you for your more than 60,000-year caring custodianship of this land which, we the invaders now all call home. I am deeply sorry!

It is this unconscious shadow of self-loathing that we project and it acts to detach us from ourselves and, just like wearing shoes, we place a layer of artificiality be-tween us and our biology of primordial existence. Organic is what we physically are – we cannot escape that. Any delusion of escapism in this sense is suicidal.

Through artificiality, no matter what form it takes, whether AI technology, plastics, synthetics, pesticides, to name a few poisons we attack our Earth with (the same Earth that allows us to exist!) we are ultimately attacking ourselves and the biodiversity we are part of with these poisons. Wake up – we are not separate from the Earth.

In the long term, artificiality is unsustainable as it is not self-regenerative and exists at the expense of the bio-diverse sphere which we are also a part of and rely on. We use the organic world to create inorganic substances that are soul destroying and anti-life. The organic world is our soul, our life source and life force – the gift of life organic technology created for all life on Earth which has sustained us for billions of years.

Science technology has tapped into and infiltrated the electromagnetic wave energy of the universal energy to create artificial and invasive waves of communication, causing disturbances and blockages in the space around us, restricting our access to the energy gifted to us by or-ganic technology to guide and centre us. Our devices now speak to us like prophets of knowledge guiding us through the electromagnetic field usurped by the CRAP system from 'organic-transmission' technology.

To stay sane in this bombardment of science technology it would be wise to take regular and long breaks from technology to adjust and counteract the incremental harmful effects from artificial communication technolo-gy, or we will lose our health and our sanity. If we haven't already!

The more technology we need and use, the more space it takes in storage facilities to save all that data. The data industry is very fast growing and not only does it need an enormous amount of water and electricity, it also needs an enormous amount of space to house the ever-growing number of computers in which to store our data. The carbon footprint of data storage contributes massively to the overall greenhouse gas emissions of the planet. The environmental price we pay for its existence is mind-boggling.

Inform yourselves and start to reduce the data you create – beginning with all those photos you take of yourselves, as they are data and need to be stored somewhere. Get up, get wise and get acting for organic life.

> *'I fear the day that technology will surpass our human in-teraction. The world will have a generation of idiots.'*
>
> *Albert Einstein*

Our second projected shadow is that primordial-ness is stagnant, primitive and lacking in wisdom. This perpetuates the deluded notion that the insatiable drive for so-called advancement and progress will make us live better, live longer, be more powerful and make us more intelligent than our image of the primordial human. However, intelligence without wisdom is exactly what we have become and intelligence without wisdom is foolishness and stupidity itself.

Advancement and progress only destroys the organic biodiversity and creates itself into an artificial entity that advances and progresses the planet and all living beings into a state of constant damage control to the point of no return. The intelligence which comes from the obtusity of our lack of wisdom is to not only destroy biodiversity but, at our worst, we manipulate organics to annihilate other homo sapiens with biological and nuclear warfare, where the only survival possible in the short term is artificiality.

Even our food sources are being replaced with artificial products. These foods resemble the real thing to convince us that we're eating a healthy alternative and that we are safe because we are finding solutions to feed our growing, already overpopulated, world. Unfortunately, these substitutes only take us further and further from our source. Obtusity has a short-term memory because it fails to connect cause and effect. When we consider all of our past disasters made by scientific tampering of our environment, how can we think that our intelligence makes us wise and that knowledge gives us power and a future. Seriously, what do we do with all that knowledge and power? We create weapons of mass destruction as a so-called deterrent and make them available to every despot. I shake my head in disbelief!

Wisdom is earnt, not created, and it is in the domain of organic technology which has sustained itself for billions of life-giving years.

Stupidity is thinking that artificial technology, which has been in existence for maybe a century, is going to be long-term life-giving – and we put our faith and our future in this dead inorganic technology. How stupidly desperate are we to not see this?

The huwoman is aware that wisdom is earned, and when earned, it is a gift to be shared with her community and the huwoman child who through inherited genetic makeup is born knowing all her ancestors' accumulated experiences. Imagine not having to go through the teenage years – what a blessing! The huwoman child is guided by her adult community to use her gift of wisdom wisely.

The third shadow we project, which belongs mainly to the male aspect of our duality, is we live in a patriarchy where the dominant power is the aspect of our species which cannot give birth of itself but needs the all-powerful life-giving woman to do so. Only in her can he create the image of himself. How preposterous! Women are the vehicle for his survival. Therefore, to ensure his survival, her survival must be controlled because the creative power of giving birth to oneself, and in the image of oneself, is the ultimate creation. In our perception the all-powerful male God himself is the only one able to do this.

The whole and sole purpose of the patriarchy is to oppress women and elevate men and their egos. The powers which make up the trinity of patriarchy, capitalism and religion has been encouraging this deception for more than 2000 years to the point of eventual destruction of our biodiverse life-giving organic planet. All just because giving birth to themselves is not possible and, in a duality, there is only life or death. If you can't create life then you must create death in order to feel powerful.

In the ego-based perception, the male of the species is seen as stronger and superior to the Goddess herself – the woman of our species – and he will show his prowess by having power and control over her through acts of violence if she does not comply to his superiority. 'How dare she create inside her and in her own image and we can't! After all, we are the all-powerful males created in the image of our god who is also male. Where is the woman in this trinity? There are no women in god's trinity. She is an imposter!'

So, the insane solution to remedy this perceived inequality and inadequacy by the male aspect of our species is to create anti-life, because in a duality there is only life and anti-life – life or death. And with that underlying psychology, the birth of technological science is born to create AI technology as a substitute and eventual replacement by the usurping of the natural act of giving birth by organic technology. Isn't this the actions of a psychology devoid of understanding the responsibilities needed for the gift of being able to give natural organic physical birth to another and working to create a healthy and sustainable world for that creation? Instead, this psychology of lack is creating an unsustainable anti-life world and we believe this trajectory is normal behaviour. Scary stuff!

Our future biology is technology by science and finite

In technological science, birth is manufactured and creates soulless inorganic entities in a crude image of ourselves. The race to create the perfect artificial woman who will perform to the male ego is here and is being refined rapidly, all for the gratification of the male's egoic disfunction which believes he is god, made in the image of god and will create woman in his image. This is the psychology of our unstoppable trajectory. We are so caught up in this delusional stupor we can no longer recognise ourselves on the journey to our self-destruction and that of the organic world which has kept us living for billions of years, without help from our artificial technology.

Unfortunately, science technology has now infiltrated the minds of our children and, contrary to our children's beliefs, they are not old enough to have acquired the wisdom to understand the consequences of their actions. The CRAP system has taken the minds of our children from us and there's nothing we can do about it – or can we???????

To recap, the three projected shadows of our underlying psychology are:
• fear of our primordial-ness
• continuous progress at any cost removes us from our primordial-ness
• the male aspect of our species with their feelings of inadequacy of not being able to reproduce themselves without the woman of our species.

Conflict is happening at our inner core and our constant warring is happening unknowingly inside of us. Thus, we create our world of conflict and disharmony based on fear and our fear destroys us and life itself.

Illusionary fear keeps us trapped in the things we fear.

I am alarmed to learn that Artificial General Intelligence (AGI) technology is being developed and progressing unimaginably fast. The aim of this AGI is to replace every human working task, because AGI can do a better job and will be cheaper. Even more alarming is that the few mad men who develop this technology are excited about being able to let AGI lose to self-govern, in self-control – no human at the helm and with no human intervention. This madness will take us to the complete loss of humanity. How does one deal with a machine who has no humanity and works on machine logic alone with a sensibility given by the mad men who control this technology?

Ironically we are creating an artificial entity who does not need to eat yet is resource hungry. We believe in and support this fantasy trajectory of evolution rather than create the imaginative reality of evolving into the psychology of the kind, caring and peaceful huwoman, waiting for us to recognise her in ourselves.

I don't know about you but the frustration I experience when trying to contact an organisation and have to deal with communicating with an AI-chatbot instead of a real person is demoralising. The demoralisation of the human race is upon us. GAIA HELP US!

I went to see The Creator (2023), a film produced and directed by Gareth Edwards. Although it was very mildly entertaining I came away thinking what a lot of expensive propaganda or should I say a 'proper gander'. Depicting that robots have inherited the kinder part of humanity and organic humanity is evil. They were also inferring that robots were programmed to not kill humans and yet there was nothing but humans and robots killing each other. If science fiction predicts the future, Gaia please help us!

Unlike AI, humanity operates in a variety of complex possibilities, driven by feelings of compassion and other emotions. Apparently there are no mistakes in AI, only logic. The biggest and most illogical mistake is creating AI in the first place, and to think that inorganic evolution is a logical trajectory. Humanity cannot exist in a machine. Once we lose humanity, we are no longer part of organic technology which has created us, but a destroyer of it and ultimately ourselves.

The frightening irony is that this technology is being developed foremost, by and for, military use – these mad men want these war machines with no humanity to be autonomous to make decisions about who they kill and what they blow up. This is the ultimate armchair entertainment computer video game for the big boys. Who says video games don't affect the psyche of (especially our male) children, to lean towards violence? When the fantasy becomes reality to be played in the field of war, we are all affected and many suffer. Get me out of here!

Artificiality is anti-life. Organic is pro-life and life itself.

The trinity of science fiction: predict – create – possibility. Does science fiction predict the future, does it create the future or does it offer possibilities for the future? The cultural in which science fiction is born from determines the predicted possibilities to be created.

∞

Without our organic senses we would literally be senseless and unable to navigate the organic world. Modern science technology is taking us further from our senses and replacing our diminishing organic senses with artificiality, which acts as another layer between ourselves and our organic-ness. One must stop and ask why this obtuse paradigm needs to recreate what has already been created by organic technology without artificial substances and science technology? This ideology of 'we can do better than organic technology' is robbing us of our senses and future life by placing us in controlled artificial environments where the use of our senses becomes obsolete and dangerously leaves us senseless.

What they try to achieve artificially and in a destructive way, we have already been given by the wonders of the sustainable organic technology. We only need to look at what it has given us to date – life itself. Wow! And we want to destroy this. What kind of sanity is that? It's the furthest from sanity we can be. Let's stop the war on organics, because in this war, there are no winners and at the point when there is no winner, organics will survive. But at what cost?

Humans in general are sleepwalking, avoid taking responsibility for their actions, blame others for their doings and find it very difficult to reach the inner depths of their true psychology because this culture discourages it. It is still considered self-indulgent to spend time on one's own, especially as a woman, to contemplate and reflect on oneself for better understanding of one's inner and collective psychology.

Any system which tampers with its own organic nature has a very deep self-hatred, while at the same time is in the delusional game of playing god in the image of the male god they have invented. Again, scary stuff! To want to replace themselves with artificiality because they think they will be able to control and remove nature out of themselves is ludicrous and ultimately impossible and unsustainable. When those who control our capitalist economic system don't need organic sensory entities to create the completed artificial entity, catastrophe and unimaginable suffering will prevail.

What makes me laugh is that when the capitalist economic controllers are about to introduce something, which is going to be very lucrative but detrimental in the long term to the organic sensory sleepwalker's future, they run under the banner of 'aiding humanity'. It is said that this technology will make us better off and we believe them. They never tell us about the consequences. Why is that? Is it because they don't want to know or they don't care? It seems that as long as there is money to be made and status to be gained there are no bounds to their deception.

How can an eight billion (and growing) population be better off when they have been replaced by an inorganic senseless replica of themselves? What are all these people going to do without a monetary way of survival? And with the natural environment severely compromised, what are they going to eat?

They say AI will give us more time to create! Dispossessed people are generally in fear and the only creating happening in the future is unspeakable upheaval and suffering which will come upon the sensually born. This catastrophe will be controlled by their senseless replacements who are not guided by organic sensory sensibility but controlled by an outside force governed by the capitalist economic powerfools' fantasies.

The more tampered we are with artificiality, the more our senses diminish in capability. We are then rendered redundant and unable to survive in the organic world our home. We then become more and more reliant on artificiality, the very thing which is killing us. The human of the very near future will be giving away their body, soul and spirit – therefore their power – while sleepwalking. As stated, the capitalist powerfools have control of the minds of our children who are not yet wise enough to make sensible decisions for themselves.

We have age requirements to have sex, vote and drive a car, yet children have free access to the madness of the internet created by science technology. We are handing our children over in the same style as child trafficking, only for free, to the powerfools of the capitalist economy.

Interestingly, the artificials:
• do not eat but they are organic resource hungry
• do not easily, if at all, organically decompose and instead, pollute organic life
• cannot give birth to themselves and rely on organics to regenerate and create more evolved versions of themselves.

This is the psychology of the capitalist trade economy where anything goes and everything is for trade at a price. Even the priceless organic human life is for sale and unlike child trafficking, we are not only just giving our children away for free, but we are paying for that privilege with our lives. Do I really need to say any more to have your attention?

You may laugh and use words, such as, poppycock, this is big brother conspiracy theory stuff. That may be so. However, the capitalist economic powerfools may be too obtuse, self-possessed and self-obsessed to see the consequences of their actions because the dollar is more important to them than life itself. However, I find this even harder to believe and it does not change the fact that this is our imminent trajectory if we do not wake up, take action, consciously reduce our population and project ourselves into the **huwoman psychology** of caring for each other, our planet and living in peaceful kindness.

The huwoman is part of and is in awareness of her organic universe. There is nothing greater. Stop and look around you. Look above you and into the night. Wow! We are part of that technology of organics – what more can one need?

Artificiality means: made by humans to copy something that occurs naturally. Why in Gaia's name would we want to copy ourselves when we are organic perfection? This psychology is made of fantasy and is the antithesis of organic and sustaining life.

Why destroy life to make an artificial object animate when we are already organic animation in motion? Is artificiality not the psychology of madness? Is this not the psychology of an entity that views being able to give birth with envy, an entity that needs to shed another's blood due to menstruation envy, an entity with an inferiority complex so great that to feel self-important it must power over, control, destroy and kill to feel? If you can't give birth you must kill – the duality of the CRAP system. After all, other than menstruation and childbirth, the only way to shed blood is to hurt or be hurt. The huwoman is in the flow of organic technology. Whereas the human is in the flow of the artificial technology created by ego-based capitalist science built from fantasy.

Most of us, deny or reject our primordial-ness, especially in the west. The evils of the duality system have taken possession and we go along because we think we are powerless to stop it, because we need stuff and we need to eat. Whereas the primordial looking huwoman made of organic technology, will enjoy, cherish and appreciate the sensualness of being alive and experience life through her highly attuned senses, where the mind and thoughts combine in harmony rather than be at odds.

The huwoman is connected to her senses and understands that she is sensual and not as vehicles of flights of fantasy; her sensuality is no longer sexual but is the vehicle by which enhances her awareness of being alive, knowing she belongs, is connected and inseparable from all that is. If we don't destroy our planet, the huwoman will emerge by necessity as a future evolution – this is already happening, slowly and incrementally and is therefore going unnoticed. Hopefully, as she becomes fully emerged, at the same time there will be a shift in cultural awareness and we will recognise her, rather than ostracise her.

In the highly likely case that we cause an unnatural apocalypse, hopefully enough will survive for evolution to take its imaginative and kind hand to reinvent and project us into the highly evolved and civilised huwoman, for the continuation and longevity of our amazing species.

I highly recommend watching Earth a 2023 miniseries on ABC iview presented by Chris Packham, produced by BBC Studios. It is a very moving documentary showing the incredibly imaginative evolutions of our 4.5 billion-year-old planet, demonstrating the astonishing lengths Earth has undergone to create life and house the life she has created. With this documentary in mind a huwoman evolution is but a cinch in the imaginative capabilities needed in developing a huwoman future of existence based on peace, harmony and kindness.

Community

A community unpacked = common-unity, and in the not so common unity of our world there is a lot of woe at the moment. This got me thinking about the importance of creating a community and being in community. It is, I think important to belong to a number of communities outside family and creating community and getting to know the people in one's own neighbourhood is essential for a healthy and safe community-minded neighbourhood. There are many activities one can do to bring the neighbourhood together, for example, a food swap, a creative activity or just a bring a plate to share get together in someone's garage or the local park every so often.

There are many things that keep a community healthy. At the heart of it is being able to relate to each other with kindness and respect; then everything else will fall into place.

In a community, we don't all need to be friends or have the same politics but we do need to be friendly and caring. In a community there are many possibilities for developing friendships and these friendships may change in intensity at different times. Accepting these changes with friendliness and kindness is what makes a community strong. For the huwoman, a community filled with friendship, caring and kindness is where she lives. Her psychology is wired by electro-magnetic impulses which trigger kindness passed on to her by the wisdom of her kin. The huwoman lives in the wisdom of her ancestry and not in the shadow of, nor in fear of, her ancestry. She knows her organic primordial-ness is her core yet is able to act and think outside her biology without destroying herself and the biodiversity of her home.

Unlike our dual system she will be empowered by her primordial-ness and yet not be motivated by the same psychology as ours, because she is fully sustainable and does not need anything other than natural light to survive. In this regard, she will take primordial thinking to a new evolution by uniting the mind, senses and thought to exist in their fullness within her. Thought then becomes an ally rather than an enemy of her mind and together they act in harmony, promoting longevity of survival by allowing organic technology to do what it does best – create and sustain life.

If we don't reinvent ourselves now and head back towards our original organic technology, then the technology of sciences will become our biology and the future human will be replaced and implanted with artificiality, that which is inorganic and anti-nature. The only fully sustainable building block is made from organic technology and cannot be replaced with anti-nature technology.

Backwards in wisdom

I hear people say, we can't go backwards, as if saving our planet, reconnecting with our planet and ourselves is a backwards step. I ask again, who are we?

Anyone with any sort of wisdom knows that there are times when it is necessary to stop, take a step back, and seriously reflect before taking a forward step. Linear is conceptual and of duality. Life moves in a circular motion, regularly stopping, sometimes appearing to go backwards, and taking time to reflect along the way as a process for gaining wisdom and clarity.

The most important step backwards we must take for our survival right now is to take our population back to the more sustainable 1950 levels of approximately two billion people. That step backwards allows us to go forwards in wisdom and to take responsibility for our survival and the survival of future generations. In seventy or so years, we have gone from being human to becoming a deadly virus and the only medication we have are the medications that sustain the virus.

The huwoman can only reproduce herself once maintaining a stable population in harmony with the surroundings of her planet.

From homo-sapiens = wise human to homo-virus = infective agent in 70 years.

∞

Organic is in the wisdom of perfection. Artificiality is in the folly of fantasy. Our senses empower us, artificiality disempowers us and puts us in the way of the dangers of fantasy, with the belief that artificiality created by technological science will make us progressive and powerful. Power in the hands of the unwise and driven by capitalism puts us in the way (to say the least) of harm and at the helm of a very precarious future.

It is imperative that we wake up from our stupor, unshackle ourselves and each other from the CRAP system for the sake of our children, grandchildren and our planet. For without our planet we are homeless and lifeless. We must reclaim our primordial-ness, imagine and create new role models based on harmony which comes from caring, kindness and the life-giving practices that organic technology affords us.

If we are to win this war against our own destruction and have a chance at survival we must accept and cherish our primordial organic ingenuity, reduce our human population drastically, salvage the biodiversity that keeps our planet alive, work together with and in our communities to support each other to transition humanity from becoming disconnected with life and being replaced artificially.

Taking moments of time to reflect, rather than react, is transforming and will help us sound the language of peace. One reflects by asking oneself – what is the best course of action for oneself and the planet at the same time? If your action is pro-organic, it is pro-planet, pro-us and pro-the creative power of organic technology. Any action which is pro-artificial fantasy is anti-us, anti-planet and ultimately anti-universe and the universe is us. I say organics forever!

In the trinity of the presence of time

Most of us live in the past and in the future even when we are in the present. Past, present and future is the trinity of time. The present creates the past and the future. The present, past and future create each other simultaneously. Past, present and future appear to be linear but move in a circular manner, are interconnected and only exist by an ability to be conceptual; but in universal reality there is only now.

In the moment, the past and future are also present in thought – being in awareness of these thoughts is not to dwell on them because what they are is thoughts and often thoughts stemming from fear of both past and future. Thank them for their insight stemming from past memories and for their suggestion of future possibilities, then return to the present and what is actually happening right now in this moment.

It is wise to acknowledge the past and future possibilities but to dwell in these thoughts is not helpful. To be in the wisdom of the moment is to know that what you do right now will shape the past and the future. Be in awareness that thoughts of past and future may not be relevant to the now. In the trinity of time, awareness of thought, mindful action and recognising the consequence of our actions is to create wisely in the moment.

The past can often be like a security blanket. We hang on to it, we build structures to house it and we live by the mark it has made on us. The past is also our strength of experience, and the future is of our creation with each step we take in the moment. Be guided by the moment by trusting that you will not react in fear but respond in that moment with appropriate and thoughtful action.

To move forward from the structures of the past, we must be aware of our past, but it must not define us. The more emotional and physical structures we build around ourselves, the more responsible we feel for these structures, trapping ourselves with often unnecessary and imposed responsibilities stemming from our past.

The CRAP culture places women especially, in the position of responsibility, so much so that the burden of multitasking can take its toll in creating inner imbalance, leading to feelings of guilt and a sense of dis-ease by the structures of imposed cultural needs for security.

Observation – it is interesting that the burden of multi-tasking originally coined in the sixties as computer terminology has now been bestowed on women, once again creating a convenient excuse for the men (in particular) in their lives to receive more while doing less. Poor men they can only do one thing at a time – my heart bleeds!

Women being born and bred in the patriarchy will readily adopt a belief if it gives them an edge in service and men in that respect will give no argument. These kinds of projections shape our belief systems. I am sure that both women and men have multitasking skills, but the patriarchal machine is based on deception and the more it can get women in service of men the more it will promote that deception. Now, in the technological age, its power is limitless and there is no limit to the lengths it will go to delude for money, power and control.

The only structure the huwoman needs is the physical structure she inhabits – this allows her to move and choose freely rather than becoming entrapped by cultural expectations from a structural system built on past fears and insecurities.

The less burden from the complexities of responsibilities we have the more possibilities are open from an imaginative perspective and one is then in a position where boundaries of the past are not of entrapment, nor is past a separate entity, but integrated in the awareness that past, present and future are the revolving trinity of physical existence.

We become free from imposing structures by creating and working to be in inner harmony and balance with the structure we inhabit. In this way, like the huwoman, we are unbound, and our house is not filled with the boundaries of cultural structures but filled in the simplicity of the awareness that the possibilities of the imagination are boundless.

Learning to be in the present moment is not without thought. It is being in awareness of thought and allowing thought to pass through, while also staying alert with one's surroundings and knowing at which moment to appropriately use thought for action if necessary.

Thought is a necessary part of our survival mechanism and instinctual. It moves especially fast in a flight, freeze or fight situation. That's how we decide which one to use.

We go through life not noticing the significance of each moment and that it is the base by which we create our lives – to create our lives with significance is to notice the moment in its full potential.

Be mindful of your thoughts as they are instinctual and creative and travel via electrochemical impulses. Thoughts are very difficult to measure. It is believed they travel virtually in no time, while in physical impulse time they travel at around 70 to 120 metres per second. Light travels at 300,000 kilometres per second. The speed of sound varies according to temperature and generally travels at 1 kilometre per 2.91 seconds. Thought vibration is not as fast as light nor sound but nevertheless is a creative vibration and a real thing. Be mindful of the power of your thoughts!

When we are in the moment, between the past and the future, the way through with thoughts is to ask yourself a question:

Is what's going on in my thoughts happening physically in real time, right in this moment?

If the answer is no, then you are in virtual no time. These are flight, freeze or fight for survival thoughts that don't need to be put into action in that moment. You are caught up in the modus operandum of the deeply embedded natural brain and thought functions which are a very important part of our primordial survival skills and very necessary at times – a gift from organic technology. Acknowledge these thoughts and ascertain if they are appropriate in the moment in which you find yourself. Generally, thoughts of fear triggering our emotional state are also happening when we are on our own and obviously in no other danger than that of our thoughts.

Once you consciously bring your awareness to this fact, you then realise you are creating in virtual time. To word it another way, thoughts happening in virtual time and not happening due to a response situation in reality are creating energy and energy cannot be destroyed only reshaped. Therefore, what you create in virtual time are unwanted thought situations that place you in the way of attracting these often-unwanted thought situations in the physical future of your reality. The way through is not necessarily spending endless time in meditation, although some meditation is very helpful. It is simply to use your thought process to remind yourself in a calm manner that you are creating the seed for a future that you do not wish to create. When you do that you are released in that moment. Keep doing that forever if you have to. It's virtual, so it takes virtually no time and over time it will become an automatic reminder with little effort. Remember to be aware of your breathing and breathe deeply, as that will help clear your thoughts (another gift from organic technology) so you can go about your life in each moment afresh with a positive perspective.

The mantra, if you need one, is: 'Is my perceived danger in my fantasied thoughts or is the danger physically or emotionally happening to me right now – am I at risk in this moment?'

We can never be out of our thoughts but we can choose what to think and to reshape the images of our thoughts – and it is a choice! This is one way to bring calm and balance in the present and where positive action can be created in full awareness rather than in reaction.

In the physical we are in the trinity of the present, past and the future. The present is where past and future meet to find balance. The past creates our present and in the present we create our future with what we choose to do with our thoughts, actions and images. If the present were to have a perimeter, it would be based in the perimeter of our past, how we choose to see, think and act in the knowledge of that perimeter will determine our future.

Past, present and future is the working trinity of conceptual time and part of our manifested illusionary reality. In manifested reality one must simultaneously be aware of the past, present and future because they are not separate. They are intertwined and constantly revolving around each other in the perpetual present. To create and manifest the future, one needs to delve into the future with our imagination while in the present and in the knowing of the past. To be solely in the present is to operate without the other aspects of its trinity, creating imbalance. One must be in awareness of all aspects of the time trinity to be in harmony with the present manifestations. However, in universal reality there is no past, present or future, just creative energy in perpetual motion travelling through space – and that includes us.

The huwoman lives in the presence of full awareness of her past and creates her future peacefully and in harmonious awareness within herself and with what surrounds her in the present moment. To be in the presence of full awareness is intoxicating and is to be in Divinity itself.

In the huwoman culture, the awareness of good and bad in the present is a concept of the past created by the operations of a conflicting duality system based on fear.

Let's become the huwoman who lives in the presence of the present, unbound by the past nor restricted by the future and lives in the unifying trinity of the present.

The huwoman is graceful, grateful and gracious – the trinity of humble.

> When the moment becomes our
> past, our past is but illusion.
> Our future is but illusion,
> until the moment it becomes.
> So, if the moment becomes the past
> and the future becomes the moment,
> all is an illusion
> except the moment in itself.
> As we journey from one moment to the next,
> with no illusion to delude us,
> then the moment becomes the present,
> the precious present of life.

In the wisdom of doubt

To be truly in the moment with wisdom one must act in non-attachment. Meaning that nothing matters, and yet it does, and knowing that the outcome of any situation is acceptance of what is. Good decisions are made from non-attachment.

When in doubt, do nothing, until there is no doubt, and the way is clear. In a situation of doubt, usually the way forward is by taking direction from each moment and doing what is required of you in that moment until clarity becomes obvious.

If you're in a situation where you can't choose between one thing or the other, the third option is to choose none, but rather, find stillness in yourself until the clarity of sensibility returns and either one of the two, or a different possibility all together becomes clear. To act in doubt is to jeopardise appropriate action because when you are not clear, other people make decisions for you according to their needs. To make decisions in clarity is powerful action and will place you in the direction of your path.

Doubt is also our friend. If we do nothing while in doubt, it allows us to stop and reflect, giving us a fresh perspective before taking the next step in clarity. Wisdom is the ability to think and act with common sense using insight through inner knowing.

The trinity of gaining wisdom is learning from experience – trusting in inner knowing to make good judgements – and compassionate understanding.

The path of least resistance

What is the path of least resistance? The path of least resistance is not about taking the easy way out nor is it for the lazy in the hope to get away from being responsible. The path of least resistance is found in the path of self-awareness. Non-resistance is an action gained from the hard work of learning self-acceptance, trusting in the process of the moment and knowing that your actions are based in kindness and in the wisdom from having understood and achieved self-awareness. In self-awareness one acts as if no-one means anyone or any-thing harm and if one finds oneself in harm's way then gracefully move away.

Self-awareness and self-obsession

There is self-awareness and there is self-obsession. What is the difference between the two in the moment? Self-awareness is when one is aware of one's presence in an environment, and one is aware of one's actions and thoughts while being respectful towards that environment and situation. Being in the moment in self-awareness is the ability to observe where one is standing in their surroundings and at the same time asking, what can I see, hear and sense right now and how do I adjust to be in tune with my surrounds while maintaining integrity and respect in and for that moment? This all happens in virtual no time and thoughts informed by the mind of the senses.

The more one practices self-awareness, the more adept one will be to read the moment for wise action. Wise action comes from knowing, experiencing and understanding self-awareness. In self-awareness we don't need to look good, we feel good because we are trusting of our inner depth of knowing.

Self-obsession on the other hand is when one is obsessed with oneself, so much so that they do not notice their environment and therefore lose connection; then one acts thoughtlessly towards their environment and situation. Being in self-obsession is being wrapped up and absorbed in oneself, losing spatial awareness, needing to look good, fearing judgement and being in reaction mode. Reaction mode from self-obsession will often insight anger, hurt, wanting to be right and this does not feel good, because it is based in the superficiality of self-obsession.

In self-awareness, we respond to our environment with care, in self-obsession we react to our environment with fear.

Every moment is directive, directional and guiding. In self-awareness trust in the directional guidance of every moment and you will enter the magical world of serendipity, where events seemingly happen by chance and in one's favour. Remember nothing happens without effort. Luck and serendipity do not just fall out of the sky. We create them with our thoughts, images and actions. Finding ourselves in the right place at the right time is serendipity by culmination of our intentions and our actions. Follow the direction of the moment with acceptance and when at a crossroad use your intuition and inner guidance as direction - you will then be in the right place at the right time and you will find yourself where you want to be without a struggle.

The huwoman is fully present in her self-awareness, responds to any situation with trust in herself because she is listening, observing and absorbing her surroundings, acting in the guidance of her self-awareness and knowing that the outcome of her actions will be from the best possible intentions, allowing each moment to develop as it must.

Every moment is in the illusion of passing time. We are in a passing time illusion so that we can experience ourselves in the sensory physical form to fully appreciate ourselves and our potential for the growth of universal consciousness. We are universal consciousness in growth.

Perfection is the order of the universe.
    Serendipity is the communication of the universe.
      Energised matter is the creativity of the universe.

Together all three make up the trinity which is the intelligence and the heart consciousness of the universe.

The elder years

The CRAP over-sexualised system worships nubility and abhors the aged. Women are considered old and undesirable a lot earlier than men. Old is not desirable to the male fantasy of his virility and he fears becoming old, reminding him of his organics, diminishing prowess and mortality.

A system that does not value nor respect the aging aspect of themselves is a very poor and unbalanced system of culture that acts from a lack of wisdom and a trajectory without consideration of the long-term consequences of its actions. Again, wisdom is earnt from experience and is not generally the domain of the young. The young and the old must work together, listen to each other and combine the wisdom of age with the eagerness of youth to create a more balanced culture.

The huwoman having that balance within herself respects and understands those who have given her life and passed their wisdom on to her. I see so much disrespect for the wisdom of age, and science technology at the rate it is 'progressing' excludes older people while elevating the young so they think they know it all. To think one knows it all is never a healthy attitude in any age group, and especially in the hands of the undeveloped mind of nubility.

In recent times, I have noticed a push to have the general public onside and of course from a capitalist economic system and not from any sort of compassion or wisdom, to see our elders as an economic burden to our society. I often notice graphic images that depict the aged as needing to rely on walking sticks, wheelchairs and other aids. Not only are these images offensive to older people but also to people of varying physical abilities.

We should all be offended by such manipulating images of lack of compassion for the very people who hold the fabric of our culture together. It is these images that brainwash us to believe that our elders no longer contribute and that they are superfluous to society. I don't know about you but when I look around me, I see a lot of elders holding the fabric of society together by donating their time voluntarily, filling in the gaps where nubility won't. Our elders create communities around them and are often nearby to help with the grandchildren.

An example of the sort of contribution which goes unnoticed by the economic warlords and the 'profits of doom' is that in my area, as in many other places, retirees have volunteered their time for years to create such things as seed banks, collecting indigenous flora seeds and then propagating and planting them to revegetate areas annihilated by our carelessness. Our seed bank now also grows to supply councils and landscapers. The list of volunteer work done by our elders is endless. Start noticing and appreciating it. Kindness towards who we are, who we will become and where we belong is life-giving.

The double-edged sword of pharmaceuticals

I find it interesting that the over-prescribed and easily accessible pharmaceutical drugs have been made legal, making us think we are being healed and can live longer with their help. And statistics say, that indeed, we generally live longer now, but whether it's due to pharmaceuticals is debatable. Ironically, this coincides at a time when we are dangerously overpopulated.

In this system, our elders are seen as an economic threat due to working longer and taking up workspace in lieu of the exploitable nubility. While at the same time older people are the biggest consumers of pharmaceuticals making them very lucrative and possibly indispensable to pharmaceutical companies. Is there no end to the paradox of the CRAP system?

Pharmaceutical companies are capitalising on our fear of death by peddling slow-release life-destroying chemicals, which pass through us into the environment when we urinate etc. I wonder how the levels of cholesterol, blood sugars and metal health is going with our fish population – I hope it's helpful for them and that they are living longer too!

It is in the interest of pharmaceuticals companies to hide the very effective healing power of the placebo from us and therefore we lose the ability and the knowing that not only it exists but also the opportunity to heal ourselves. Oh, yes and there's always another pill as a counter-reaction to compensate for the harmful side effects of the original pill taken.

Placebo = the power of thought image and conviction which trigger a series of biochemical reactions in the body that promote self-healing. We don't give ourselves time to heal. We opt for a pill, and we keep going. There's a pill for just about everything these days so it's not hard. It's like alcohol. It's easily accessible and in excess not necessarily good for us.

To take a pill for just about any ailment robs us of our self-healing power. I am not saying that there are times that pharmaceuticals are not useful to aid our self-healing, such as a healing herb or remedy, but to be prescribed many-a-pollutant for the sake of it becomes a substance that we become addicted to rather than a substance which will aid in our own power to heal. We become so addicted to the drugs prescribed that we believe we cannot live without them and that we will live longer by taking them, so there is no point in trying to heal ourselves because the drugs are doing it for us. We are prescribed lifelong chemicals which deprive us of our inner ability to heal, gifted to us at birth by our organic mother nature.

A note – pharmaceuticals do not cure but they retard damaging effects over time – they are a quick fix. However, diet, exercise and lifestyle play a similar role but with the often-added bonus of healing ourselves by healthy means for ourselves and the planet. Pharmaceuticals are pushed on us with no regard to the consequences and at a cost to the future of our planet, and we readily accept this without question.

Our bodies are a tool, and like any tool, it needs to be looked after to do the job properly. Keep your body, mind and spirit healthy and they will take you a long way without external interference.

What is wrong with living to the natural lifespan of our organic organism? Why are we so afraid of death? Is it because the psychology of duality only sees life and death rather than Life, death and transition? Is the duality aspect of life and death truly final?

The lost art of the gift economy

The gift economy is a sharing system based on gift giving freely without expectation of being given something back in return. This system was part of many cultures and we have taken that idea commercialised it and applied it mostly to birthdays, weddings, religious festivals, etc.

In its true essence, the gift economy creates and gives positively on a personal and community level because:

- The act of gifting freely increases the happiness and self-esteem of individuals
- The pleasure of gifting is socially connecting
- Gifting ensures that all community members feel safe as they are taken care of no matter the circumstances
- It creates a caring and compassionate way of being.

The gift economy has many levels in building connection between communities and each other. It aides in self-esteem and pride. It makes sure that no-one is without food or companionship. Caring for each other is part of the gift economy. In the gift economy one gives with pleasure for the good and wellbeing of all, without expecting anything in return.

The gift economy does not fall within the capitalist death economy but falls within the fundamental principal of life and sustainable survival of all that exists. The principle is living in harmony with the natural environment, gifting what one can and humbly being in receipt of what is given.

In our present paradigm, we have to be economically rich to be able to gift, and our gifts are born from exploitation and often for self-gratification. However, in the gift economy, we live in the richness found within ourself and our environment. The gift economy as opposed to a trade economy creates trust, kindness and harmony. Gifting with kindness is different to our present trade economy which creates separation and inequality prevails. The trade economy is a duality system which is hierarchical and discriminating. It obliges us to compete with each for the acquisition of money to acquire the things we think we need to feel secure.

It is interesting that when we think of the word economy, we think of money, yet if we are to unpack the word economy, we can appreciate the broader meaning. Eco means the ecology and nomy relates to a specific area of knowledge. **Eco-nomy**. Let's change the meaning of economy from money-making and anti-life to the true meaning of economy, which is that of looking after our planet and its eco-nomy.

In spirit of the huwoman gift economy, here are some guidelines to consider:

• Trust in oneself and remain focused on one's inner gifts bestowed from birth and be creative with those gifts in a manner which is beneficial to all that is

• Not only gift another but accept gifts in the way that they are given where there is no judgemental thought mechanism to control what is being gifted

• Honouring every moment is a gift and to accept each gifted moment with the boldness of grace and gratitude while taking pleasure in receiving and gifting

• Live amongst one's surroundings not with attachment or expectation, but from a sharing in the ethos of kindness – a true gift

• Gifting that which feels right to give in any given moment, becoming the modus operandi, which is shared with everything and everyone

• The gift economy is built on the sharing of helpfulness which creates peace, equality and generosity.

The huwoman's philosophy of living comes from the stream of love consciousness and not from a place of neediness. The huwoman is born with a very different psychology to the evolution of humans. The huwoman's psychology is based on awareness which comes from knowing not knowledge. The huwoman walks her Earth in the fullness and boldness of her humble self.

If in the huwoman's gift economy one does not need anything then one would not need to ask for anything. What would then be appropriate gifting?

In the huwoman culture of gifting, one gifts their own resources rather than gifting objects:
• She shares her companionships
• She gives her time and energy
• She shares in a sensual way within and with others
• She gifts her time by joining others in the rearing of children and caring for and with others while at the same time caring for herself.

Personal huwoman resources include time, companionship, meeting of minds, creativity of imagination and creating together. In the huwoman culture there is no 'I am yours and you are not mine', but 'I am mine and you are yours and together we are one'. Language and ideas of possession and behaviour of ownership are replaced with the language and actions of self-reliance, yet also knowing that being able to accept support is sometimes necessary.

For example, there are two ways to use a walking stick – one provides you with support when needed and the other is to be totally reliant and dependent on it. In other words, a walking stick can be a friend and an aid or something to cling to as a dependency. The huwoman, like a walking stick, will give support but will not make herself into a walking stick of dependence nor make others dependent on her. Yet she will be dependable!

Please note – I have used the example of a walking stick as an analogy to demonstrate a point. However, for those who have lost the ability to move easily without one then a third way to use a walking sick is to accept it as a friend and an aid.

In the huwoman's gift economy she has no needs, other than to be her natural organic self who is gently powered by natural light and basks in the power of her senses and the pleasure of life itself. She is intimate, caring and connected with all that surrounds her. Such words as rape and concepts like child trafficking are no longer in her language, but in the knowing of a past evolution. Her voice is filled with the language of peace.

In our current system we are a trading economy, where we trade one thing for the other creating huge gaps of inequity between the rich and poor. It's a duality made from our need to eat for survival. Whereas a gift society has an eco-nomy based on generosity of spirit in sharing, giving and receiving, while caring for the eco-nomy of the planet.

You may not believe me because this book could be science-fiction, but our present scary economic trajectory is the real science-fiction fantasy we are operating from. The CRAP system operates in such a way as to delude, that we must continue economically in this trajectory and at this pace because there is a huge population to exploit. It is imperative we work together to reduce our population for any chance of releasing ourselves from the capitalist scientific fiction which eventually will be our demise.

And that dear people, is the underlying psychology of capitalism where the 'profits of doom' are all about creating fake substances to accumulate an artificial concept called money, to the point where what we say and do can be **fake-ly** altered and manipulated to become true. The culture of fake news and artificiality is now born and we have given it birth and allowed it to happen by compliance. This culture will tear us apart and we will lose our humanity all together. This, if it hasn't already, will take us into a trajectory where we will not know what or who to believe and our mental state will need to be controlled by administering more and more drugs called medication – or should I call it sedation. This is the death wish of an economy that has no scruples and will stop at nothing in the race to gain power and money for the men who have been the most successful. And these are the men who create our world with their fantasies. Can you really not see this trajectory?

It is from this underlying psychology we operate and agree to function in our world, and by all of us agreeing to act in this way.

Let's change it to the psychology of the small population of the huwomankind's gift economy, of being in harmony with all that exists, including ourselves because we are a gift, a gift from the technology of organics and the only thing that can take that gift away from us is the destruction of the organic biodiversity of that which gives life on this planet.

Our present obtuse system cannot see what is right in front of it. Like children it makes no connection between or does not care about cause and effect and the importance of preserving organics and organic life, even though it is organic itself. If this is not bad enough, wait until our lives are taken over by AI and AGI technology to do our work for us and fight our unnecessary wars created to assert power, control and monetary gains for those who exploit.

This obtuse system needs continuous evidence to convince itself of anything and, even when the evidence is right in front of them, they do not see it. If they don't like what they see, they will pay someone – usually a scientist – to prove otherwise, thus becoming a world of neverending and confusing evidential-mess, heading in a linear trajectory because it cannot recognise itself in that which is right in in front it and work towards preserving what gives them their life in the physical.

The organic world is seen through the lens of capitalism as something to exploit and kill. The gift economy is built on kindness, sharing with others and ourselves, so that we can survive and thrive in harmony, be at peace with each other and our planet environment. Instead, we are allowing ourselves to be used as another organic exploitation and taking no responsibility for the consequences of these actions, by and for the financial profit of the few.

I am positive that if you were to ask any woman what sort of culture she would like to live in, she would say that living in peace and in a caring, non-violent and respectful culture is where she would like to live. My friends, that describes the huwoman culture.

PART THREE

UNLOCKING THE IMAGINATIVE SPARK: THE EVOLUTION OF THE HUWOMAN BEGINS

Having described the possibility and potential of the sustainable huwoman, there are other factors which need to be addressed if her evolution is to be possible. In our present paradigm the imaginative spark required is lacking and this section addresses those factors and the importance of imagination in evolution which is required to unlock that spark.

In our present paradigm we live and create from our fantasies. Fantasy is from a thought process that stems from physical neediness, making it limited and often inspired by the attributes of lust, greed, envy, control and self-obsession – just to name a few. Fantasies have boundaries and restrictions; very few in our world live in the boundless, expansiveness of the imagination.

Imagination is being able to use our thought process in a beyond belief way and create from the expansive, boundless and altruistic realm. Imagination comes from accessing the mind which through the senses is receiving boundless energy from the infinite source to imagine beyond the physical, with attributes of universal love, kindness and expansiveness rather than from the destructive mindlessness of our fantasies without aim on our journey to self-destruction.

One example of the fantasy we live in is the wonderful 2023 film Barbie produced by LuckyChap Entertainment. It is interesting, in so much as, even after Barbie becomes aware of and is liberated from patriarchy and finds herself in a place where she can choose beyond her biology, the last image of her shows that she chooses her biology by going to a gynaecologist. She emulates a patriarchal image of women, saying women's ability to give birth is controlled and encouraged by the CRAP system to keep women trapped and dependant. The patriarchy is so powerful that she has no choice but to comply and is then integrated into the machine, body, soul and mind, and does not even realise it. Even though this film could have used this moment for change, the rest of it wonderfully illustrated the tension between men and women in the paradigm of patriarchal duality.

Maybe there is no solution to the paradox of our duality in the patriarchal fantasy images of a woman and a man? Maybe the only way out is to imagine ourselves out of it and into a huwoman evolution.

The long-suffering wife expression springs to mind, as a person who wants something desperately enough to find happiness in suffering and accepts the smallest pittance in return. The non-suffering woman is in her own power and gets on with her life. If at any time her needs are in sync with another's then she is inclusive of the other in her life while at the same time pursuing her life's interests and connections.

New word for the huwoman evolution: triadox

A triadox is a three-way paradox. It is when a paradox is united to make a third outcome, because the huwoman does not live in duality but in a trinity. Our culture is made up of dualities, and dualities have the aspect of being paradoxical. No wonder we've all gone mad.

The trinity within the huwoman/triadox is not three separate entities but starts with two separate entities united and integrated to make a third in harmony and at peace with herself. And that is the consciousness, which is within us all. If we allow ourselves to receive it, it is the energy of wonder and of life. We are matter animated in motion, within the ultimate trinity of space, energy and matter.

What is imagination?

A fantasy is created by a need, whereas imagination creates through us and with us and is all around us. We are originally made from imagination and now make ourselves from fantasy. It is this fantasy that comes between us and our imagination of the endless possibilities of self-sustaining organic technology.

The huwoman is the child of the organic world, unlike the near future human, who will be implanted and eventually be replaced with the technology of non-sustaining artificiality.

Imagination is presented to us in the form of images. The word imagine is to think in conceptual images. Aside from the physical – we need all aspects of the physical, mental, emotional and spiritual to be in harmony with the creative stream of consciousness, which means being in the light of universal love that moves through us and also is us – we also need the awareness of mind-imagination which is the spark that enables us to manifest matter into objects that appear solid… in this case, the evolution of the huwoman.

To create this evolution, it is important to create the spark in our imagination and then in our actions. Firstly, in our physical form and secondly when we transition from this life we retain the awareness of that mind image-ination and this is easier to do if our actions are aligned with our imagination before passing.

Evolution and diversity also happen as a result of the interactions between a species and their environment. Over long periods of time, species and environments continually adapt and change to create the biodiversity which promotes life. At the rate we are changing and decimating our organic environments, it is quite likely that food will be in great shortage, and to survive we will need to eat less and less. We will then create a food source which has been so extremely genetically manufactured, in desperation, to feed an unsustainable over population of humans. This will seem like a good solution, but ultimately, like everything else we create and manipulate through science technology, we will once again be adding substances which are not in tune with the Earth, creating more problems and taking us further out of balance from our life source. If we don't blow ourselves up all together, we may even have to resort to putting each other on our menu. Hopefully over time, by the imaginative intelligence of our biodiverse planet, we will evolve into the sustainable and humane natural light-powered huwoman despite our fantasies of being able to destroy, become unsustainable and believing we can survive in this delusion.

Creating the huwoman will organically evolve by changing our images from patriarchal thought images to huwoman images, reflecting the kindest, most generous part of our humanity towards ourselves and each other and our planet. Kindness arises from within and gives outwardly.

The ethereal astral plane which resides just outside the edge of our conscious awareness is where mind-imagination creates the impetus or spark for the manifestation of matter into objects that appear to be solid. At the moment there are so many images of thought fantasy in the astral plane which act like a veil of patriarchal images entrapping us in our present creation of ourselves. Thought images can either emanate from our imagination or our fantasies. If we were living in a gift economy where kindness is the operating psychology, the pleasure of giving would be the way of life. On the way to discovering the huwoman within, practising the kindness of the gift economy would help to move us forward. Taking pleasure in genuine gifting is part of our forgotten nature.

To create with imagination, one must be present in one's imaginings while at the same time be the observer of them. So, let's start imagining and acting from her psychology of kindness rather than each man for himself and who cares about anyone else in the psychology of the CRAP system. Let's give the huwoman a head start with our actions and our imagination!

'Imagination is more important than knowledge.

Knowledge is limited. Imagination encircles the world.'

Albert Einstein

At present we use the words mind, brain and thought synonymously, which is both confusing and limiting (as I will explain in a bit more detail later). Mind thought and brain are different and play different functions. Imagination is not in our thoughts nor in our brains, it is in the awareness of our mind. When our minds are fully accessed our thoughts become a conduit for what we can imagine to manifest. The awareness of mind-imagination lives in both the physical and in the universal energy that surrounds us. The physical is where the universal mind can manifest imagination into matter.

Existence is originally created by the chemistry of organic biodiversity; we continue to evolve with the awareness of mind-imagination and continue to manifest through the power of ethereal energy.

The universe continues to evolve at the same time as we continue to evolve in response to our need and its need to survive. The evolution of the universal mind contributes to our evolution and vice versa, meaning that through the evolution of animated matter the universal mind also evolves. It's a symbiotic relationship. Mind energy shapes the ethereal energy surrounding us. The ethereal has the same quality as air; we cannot see it or touch it and yet it exists. It is both essential and powerful for evolution.

Ethereal unpacked: 'E-the-real'

E = in mathematical terms, the base of the natural logarithm. The value at 1 and the symbol ex is also the sum of the infinite series.

The real = actually existing as a thing

Therefore, ethereal energy = the base of the infinite reality of existence and of the realm of the imagination.

Unfortunately, we currently create ourselves through thought fantasy. The mind images or thought fantasies (depending on our level of awareness) that we place in the ethereal, take form in the visual realm of the astral plane as a template for creating our continuing evolution.

The astral plane which resides just outside the edge of our conscious awareness is where the ethereality of mind-imagination creates the impetus or spark for the manifestation of matter into objects that appear to be solid and through which we continue to create ourselves into the many evolutionary stages of our existence (more on creating in the astral to come).

The spirit is the presence of the universe within us. It is the spark or driver of our physical form and is the vehicle for imaginative consciousness. The spirit is connected to the non-physical realm of creation and the clearer and more complete our imaginative images are, the more likely and the quicker we are able to manifest them in the physical.

Just like the symbiotic relationship between species and environments to create biodiversity to evolve and sustain each other, so are the physical and spirit in a symbiotic relationship to aid evolution from the imagination into the physical realm.

Highly attuned awareness of the mind, highly attuned senses and highly attuned imagination describes deity. Another trinity!

Thought and imagery

Thought and imagery are energy, and once released, they cannot be destroyed and have to go somewhere. Where do they go? As we are mostly unaware of the power of our thoughts and imagery, we don't realise that it is energy in motion and travels. It travels into the space of the ethereal astral plane. There it swirls all around us (and everything else) upholding the thought images of that culture. This is our personal and cultural shadow; it weighs heavy and drains us.

At present we mostly use thought to process our physical and the psychological. If we were to learn to use thought with the mind, so that they worked together, it would look something like this:

When mind and thought are fully present with the senses and all three are working together, then we become sensual sense and we can make sense. This sensibility is not a ball of flight, fight or freeze reaction and is more in tune with its surroundings, where action comes from the wisdom that comes from knowing. Thought that comes from wisdom is sensitive, sensual and sensible, rather than thought that comes from fear which is our present primordial instinct reaction passed on to us as a shadow to carry from our ancestors.

When fully in our senses and sensual, we are not sexual, ego-centred or sentimental, but sensitive and sensible. We are not insensitive or irrational and we remain connected to the vibrations which are around us. We become part of the harmony of those vibrations and they are sensitive and in harmony with our vibration as well. We can then tap into that harmonious vibration of universal kindness, which flows through and is all around us. Some people experience this universal kindness as a yellow, red, orange vibration. The loving boundlessness is in the orange light made from red and yellow, which for some people can appear gold at times.

Being in tune with that universal light vibration has the same feeling as walking in constant sunshine no matter how grey and cloudy the day may be. Being in the universal orange light of constant warmth is what the huwoman experiences within herself and in what surrounds her. Who wouldn't want that?

Our senses are diminishing because we no longer rely on them to survive, therefore they are not as acute, so in effect our thinking capacity is also diminished and triggers the fight, freeze or flight mechanism, even when not needed, thus creating imbalance in the physical and psychological states.

Acting consciously from the fully sensory dimension of the mind is actionary based on knowing, and stems from wisdom, not fear which is reactionary. Fear is what we create when we lose touch with our mind and senses; then thought becomes louder than mind.

The more technology interferes with our biology, the more our thoughts replace our sensual minds and we move around constantly in reaction (re-action meaning mindlessly doing the same thing over and over again and expecting a different outcome). When fully responding with one's senses we are acting with mindfulness. Being fully in our senses is to be omnipresent because awareness of our surrounding is enhanced. Artificial technology is a platform for dulling and man-i-pulating our senses, allowing ourselves to be mindlessly controlled and making us victims of our own doing.

Respond-ability rather than react-ability.

As I've said before, knowing is awareness. And knowledge is fabricated! The astral space is filled with thought images of our ancestral past and these are difficult to move or penetrate because we are born imbued with them. Generationally, these are passed on and our psychology is born wired by these thought images without our awareness. It takes conscious awareness and effort to change these thought images created in the more than 2000-year reign of the trinity based on capitalism, religion and patriarchy.

To change thought images in the astral space, we must change our own thought image of ourselves. I vote that we change our images of ourselves to become the huwoman as outlined in this book, born and wired through our thought image of kindness, because to be kind is to be kindred and to be kindred is to be connected. When we are kind, kindred and connected we create the primordial psychology of the huwoman.

Making sense of the mind, sixth sense, the brain and thought

The huwoman is aware of and feels the essence of her created physical energy, because she is one with that energy flowing through and around her. She knows and understands that we are energy in motion, in a physical form, so that we can through the senses experience the pleasure of being alive. To be in touch with the energy of the senses (including the sixth) plays a major role in everyday perception and enjoyment.

The new and refined evolution of our species, the huwoman, is strongly connected to the sixth sense and is fully realised in this incarnation. Not from knowledge (something one knows intellectually) but from knowing (something one knows from the core of their being) that while in the physical all appears separate and individualised, everything is actually connected and therefore each action corresponds with its consequences – not only to the one but to all that is.

The sixth sense is our natural ability to know instinctively and is usually attributed to women. It is part of ourselves and due to our limited perception we deny it because we cannot easily perceive it. We are not taught how to access the sixth sense so it is hard to prove. We push it into the too-hard basket and pretend it does not exist.

The sixth sense and the mind play an important role in being in full awareness. We will never reach complete sensibility until we acknowledge the existence of and learn to use the sixth sense. The senses, including the sixth, are connected to and trigger the mind which then triggers the brain, which triggers instinctive thought into operation, giving us the edge for survival through the process of thought.

When our senses are diminished and the sixth sense is denied, thought becomes connected to the ego and is loud, domineering and thinks it is right. Because we are currently operating in a state where the sixth sense is suppressed, thought can be in total control, fears the unknown and becomes delusional and dangerous to the individual and the human race.

When we deny what completes us, how will we ever find our inner harmony? We spend so much of our lifetime avoiding our deeper selves, leaving us vulnerable to outside influences that give us directions on how to live. This is how the paradigm in which we live, and have lived for thousands of years, has been created and maintained through denial and fear administered by the dominant power. It is in this dominant trinity which acts as duality and duel-ality where capitalism, religion and patriarchy – the CRAP system – and power lies, that we have worshiped and obeyed.

In our culture, women are attributed to having intuition and a sixth sense. But because women in our culture are not valued, therefore intuition is not valued and is even ridiculed.

As a result, intuition has to be developed in secret, which moves us further in the dark ages.

When we deny that which we instinctively know to be true, we deny the essence of our very core, limiting our ability to a sense perception from a deeper level.

Mind, brain, thought

We treat the mind, brain and thought as synonymous. We wrongly attribute the mind to being a brain function of thought – whereas the mind exists in every cell of our bodies including the brain. The mind holds not only our conscious and subconscious memories, but also our collective unconscious, that which we bring with us from birth.

The brain is purely a highly refined and complex chemical producing machine used to process stimuli from our environment through our senses to inform thought intended for action. The brain is a machine and cannot comprehend the complexities of the mind because it is linked with thought – and thought, when disconnected from the mind, operates in ego mode mentality and this creates the unsustainable situation we are in today.

Thought is part of our physical process and is the domain of the brain. Survival would not be possible without a thought process for the function and organisa-

tion of processing information from the senses to acti-
vate the fight, freeze or flight reaction. Without a
thought process, the ability to retain and reflect on the
learning of skills necessary for physical survival would
not be possible – it would be like leaving a baby to survive on its own without any skills, only to result in an
early death.

In our current cultural paradigm, thought can be the enemy of the mind and of the imagination. It is often
caught up in the fantasy of the physical and the fear of
danger and readily awaits flight, freeze or fight, even
when in no immediate danger – it is our primordial in-
heritance. Whereas the huwoman looks primordial but
her primordial psychology is very different to ours. She is
not governed nor restricted by the primordial-ness of our
present evolution simply because she is fully self-
sustainable, making her non-predatory and therefore
non-violent in nature.

Thought, being a mechanism of our survival system, is
judgemental in nature and is there to assess, discriminate
and promote action for survival. To change a thought
process with intention, one must redirect thought energy
from judgemental to self-awareness, from discrimination
to acceptance and to be peaceful and thoughtful in one's
action. In other words, to know and understand the difference between thought discrimination necessary for

survival and when discrimination is fear-based and judgemental just because something or someone is different from our normal experience.

The mind and thought need to cooperate to trigger imagination, because without imagination we end up doing and thinking the same things over and again, until thought becomes stagnant, unimaginative, repetitive and the rot sets in. This makes fending for ourselves reliant on external systems, such as, capitalism, religion and patriarchy – the trinity which dominates our world – believing it is a duality, which in reality is a duel-ality.

In the balanced individual, the mind as well as the brain, informs thought and then thought informs the mind, and together they create harmony. Our imagination is then triggered and our fantasies begin to be recognised as delusional, limited and based on the ego-based thought process rooted in lust, greed, envy and self-obsession. The mind is our inner essence, quietly speaking to us but difficult to hear above the noise of fear that our ego-based thoughts indulge in. This separates us from our inner sense, making the position of full sense and sensibility unreachable.

Brain thought alone restricts the mind of imagination because one (the brain) is for physical survival and the other (the mind) is for connection to our inner spiritual and emotional wellbeing for harmonious survival. At present we don't accept or understand the trinity of mind, thought and imagination. We have a culture living in the 'fear thought fantasy paradigm' where mental illness and confusion becomes common.

In general, depression is associated with fear coming from the past and anxiety is associated with fear of the future – the unknown.

∞

We say – 'You are out of your mind' rather than what seems more accurate to say, 'You are out of your thoughts' – however, on second thoughts, being out of our minds is truly accurate because we are disconnected from our minds and achieving being out of our thoughts would allow room to hear the mind and give us relief from the noise. Being in tune with your senses is an essential part in informing the mind, as well as the brain, for processing into something we can understand through thought.

The duality of duel-ality

In our present paradigm, we are governed by duality – black and white, woman and man, good and evil, and so on. We believe opposites are balanced and say, 'opposites attract'. However, our illusion of duality splits us apart, rather than connects us. I find it interesting that even though spelt slightly differently, the words **dual** and **duel** sound the same and have a connected meaning. A duality, like a duel, consists of two at odds with itself.

> Dual – consisting of two separate unconnected parts.
> Duel – is two opposing factions in a contest to determine a winner.

Consequently, our present concept of a dual system is in a constant duel with organic technology for dominance. In our current culture even though we believe we live in duality, we are actually in a trinity. We operate in dualism, but in reality that dualism sits within a trinity which is capitalism religion and patriarchy. Each component of that trinity is in itself a dualism: capitalism is poor and rich; religion is good and evil; patriarchy is man and woman.

To change those into a sane, functioning and balanced operating trinity, capitalism would become the gift economy, religion would become peaceful spirituality and patriarchy would become the huwoman.

The gift economy – in huwoman harmony – in peaceful spirituality = the paradigm of the huwoman.

We deny the trinity because our limited imaginings cannot perceive it and when we cannot perceive it with our intellect, then it does not exist.

Duality is conceptual and because humans can conceptualise we can create concepts such as good and evil. We can also manifest good and evil in the physical. In other words, we create good and evil and give them life by accepting they exist and therefore create them. We are so deluded, not only by our own limitations but also by the ones we believe to be knowledgeable, because we have been deprived of feeling comfortable to develop and express our intellect through the mind and no longer know how to do it.

To imagine ourselves out of our current situation we need to create new images for our world which are not based on fantasies. It means replacing our fantasies with images coming from a will to live in future harmony – harmony meaning in the perfection of organic technology.

Imagination is image-based and just like we can choose to change our thoughts we can also choose to change the images of our thoughts and of our selves. The huwoman is offering a new image, and for her to come into being we must start acting like her. Then we change all those ancestral images that hover around us, shadowing our psychology with the primordial consciousness of flight, freeze or fight for survival, even when we are in no physical danger. If we continue to believe that artificiality, continual progress and disconnection from the natural environment will free us from our present primordial psychology that is the ultimate in the delusional fantasy of fantasies!

Let's evolve into a new primordial consciousness where primordial thinking is based in kindness, in being present in the moment, in full awareness of ourselves and our surroundings, and in knowing that we are all connected in the universe. We are the universe and live due to the universe. We owe this gift of animated life in motion to our universe. Let's become humble in appreciation of this gift and use it to preserve organic life instead of destroying it. How fortunate are we to even have this opportunity to recreate ourselves!

The trinity of our universe

To be in trinity with oneself, one's surroundings and one's spirituality is to reflect the fundamental trinity of the universe itself, space-energy-matter, which we all originate from. Therefore, to be in balance and harmony, the trinity is an important aspect of the huwoman paradigm, or any paradigm.

Duality is oppositional, whereas trinity is harmony. In my thoughts, a duality is a continuum of two extremes which can move in and out depending on attraction and repulsion and it is represented in the shape of a line. The trinity is represented in the shape of a triangle within a circle. This shape allows balance and continual self-adjustment. An example of a duality becoming a trinity comes with this question – what's between white and black? We all know it's dull old grey and yet grey is the meeting point of its trinity. Grey is the perfect canvas, the colour on which other colours can shine. When colours have grey as a commonality they are tempered, more harmonious, gentler and visually kinder with each other. Grey is the point at which the trinity canvas for possibility is made, and that grey canvas is ready and open to all possibilities.

A trinity consciousness cannot happen without a duality to start with. Duality is a stage of evolution and finite, whereas trinity consciousness is complete within itself and boundless because it revolves – everything in a trinity is always in and at the centre of itself. The trouble with duality is that it always sees itself as separate, whereas a trinity is in constant revolution and connected to itself creating balance. Every structure needs at least three points of balance otherwise it collapses.

Duality implies a connection, a partnership, but unless there is a uniting aspect (a third party known as a trinity) duality is actually a separating force, needing the third to harmonise. In our current paradigm of duality, we live in constant contradiction, a paradox. We want to be individual but more than anything we want to be partnered. Whereas the huwoman lives in a community of mutuality and reciprocity. In this society the trinity of capitalism, religion and patriarchy are replaced with the trinity of gift economy, spirituality and huwomanty.

Here's an example of a trinity at work: if red and yellow aren't combined, each remains a separate and standalone colour and not connected to each other. Whereas if we were to combine red and yellow, this creates a unity and an overlap of colours that blend to become orange. The depth and intensity of the orange created depends on the amount used from each of the original so to speak parent colours. That is the beauty and the power of the trinity, it allows for variation in its creative and uniting aspect.

The trinity of organic colour is RED – BLUE – YELLOW while the trinity of light colour is RED – BLUE – GREEN. These are the source of all colours. It is only in the overlap of these three primary colours where we see the spectrum of colour.

Similar to the example above, women and men are of the same species, not separate, and yet they are. In the sustainable huwoman what we attribute to the male of the species as masculinity is combined with the female feminine of our species to create a third in a unifying blend where both aspects meet to create balance. It's not a dilution, but a blending, to better equip us for sustainable living, by making a genetically stronger single third from the present duality.

The trinity of our future survival = Woman – Man – Huwoman.

Our masculine and feminine is separated by role play that makes for good television but little to no sense for long-term survival. The combined third allows for a more varied palette of skills which are not divvied up but shared in unity rather than separation. Separation obliges us to trade for unity which becomes hierarchical and competitive, where inequality prevails.

Does this not sound like the operating manner of the CRAP system?

I find the expression, 'things come in threes' interesting. This expression originates from the Latin phrase – 'omne trium perfectum' – meaning everything that is a set of three is perfect. The Greeks also knew of the power of three – their word is hendiatris, meaning one through three is a figure of speech used to express an idea. There are so many facts and expressions using the rule of three.

Survival comes in three =
3 minutes without air, 3 days without water, 3 weeks without
food.

In psychology, the rule of three applies in that ideas given in three ways are more interesting and memorable:
• life liberty happiness
• blood sweat tears
• breakfast lunch dinner
• lights camera action
• Earth water air
• past present future
• protons neutrons electrons

… the list goes on and on and on.

Highly attuned awareness of mind, highly attuned senses and highly attuned imagination describes deity. Another trinity! The good things that come in threes list is almost endless.

Like everything else, we have changed the original interpretation of positive things come in threes, to also include negative things come in threes – what a surprise! We have managed to turn a positive trinity into a duality of positive and negative. The huwoman is in herself a trinity – female-male-huwoman – the unifying third aspect created by the overlap, where good things come in threes. Or in this case, all things created to make a third is perfection.

When anything is in a trinity it is in harmony. When it is in a duality it is opposing. When you next find yourself at odds with a duality, use the trinity as a tool to balance the situation. Meaning, find the third possibility based in kindness, caring and with integrity. In a trinity, all aspects are at the centre making it revolve and because each aspect is in the centre, the trinity is always connected to its aspects. That is why a trinity is in balance and in harmony.

It takes two to tangle and three to untangle.

∞

I have noticed that generally when one hears something for the first time, they don't absorb it, and if they hear it a second time, they think they've heard it for the first time. But if they hear it for the third time it will be, aha! And if they hear it from a man rather than a woman — this goes for women as well — they will take notice and attribute the information to the man, even though it may have originated from a woman. Misogyny lies deep in our veins, is all around us and yet mostly goes unnoticed.

Three six nine trinity

From a numerological perspective the 3,6,9 trinity play a role in connecting with and visually understanding the trinity.

- The number 9 is associated with spiritual growth and knowledge. It is also considered an important number in the mythology of many cultures.

- The number 6 is associated with being sympathetic, gentle and loving.
- The number 3 is the omen of creativity, communication and optimism.

We may consider mythology, astrology and numerology a lot of hogwash. However, they are a language of observational wisdom passed on to us from the cultures of our past where the mind-numbing technology of our present did not exist. Even though the exclusive and reductionist methods of modern-day science looks upon ancient wisdom with disbelief, the reason this ancient language of wisdom still exists and still used by many in our time is because it still plays an important role in understanding from an inner depth, connecting to our deeper knowing and driving spirit of ourselves and the universe.

The universe operates in trinities, for example: space, energy and matter is the fundamental base of all creation. Water, earth and air is the trinity of our planet. Red, blue and yellow are the base from which all colours are created. Red, blue and green are the base colours of light. The list is endless.

In numerical terms, nine is the end and the beginning. It is a number of power and it stands alone as the last number and as the number by which multiplication of all the other numbers follow. Nine is made up of 3 x 3 x 3. Nine is the number which holds the 3 x 3 x 3 trinity.

Nine is magical if you add any other number to it, then add the result to itself it will come back to the number you added to 9. For example: $9 + 8 = 17 = 1 + 7 = 8$

Also, if you multiply a number by nine and then add the result to itself it will always come back to nine. And nine, when continuously linked to itself, creates the shape of a spiral and the revolving universe.

From a visual perspective six holds a duality of three. Nine holds the trinity of three, and yet, six and nine are visually interchangeable depending on which side one is looking from. In the deluded CRAP system, we are looking at nine from a six perspective and thwarting the full expression of a healthy trinity of three held by nine.

The reason the CRAP system's trinity is out of whack is because it operates in a culture of duality therefore, it separates and is never in balance. It has a missing leg, creating an imbalance and eventual collapse. For a trinity to work in balance, it must exist as a trinity within a trinity within a trinity and the number nine houses that trinity which is aligned and in alignment with the universe, including with its shape.

The huwoman is not in any delusion – she lives facing in the direction of the nine and operates within the trinity in its balanced fullness.

Space – energy – matter

We exist because we are made from the three fundamental aspects of the universe: space, energy, matter. I find that mind-blowing. In fact, I am in awe of everything to do with our organic, majestic universe. The diversity it sustains and that drive to reach excellence through the process of evolution is mind-blowing. The universe is our kin and therefore we have the same qualities – we are organic, diverse and we strive for excellence.

However, in our present black and white reductionist paradigm we have become disconnected from the magic of our own awesomeness and abilities to consciously create ourselves anew. We feel alone, and yet we are surrounded by others, we search for connection and yet we are part of and connected to the vastness of our universe – as awesome as that may seem we are the universe and feelings of disconnection are a consequence of the gift of having conceptual abilities and these conceptual abilities being coloured by our present system of fear and disconnection.

Let's define the three aspects we (and the universe) are made of.
• Space is where we live and what we move in; without space there is no room for existence – energy is the crea-

tive force of imaginative awareness by which everything is created and animated – matter is what energy creates with.

• Energy operates in infinity so there is no limit to possibilities; it is only limited by its imaginative awareness to manipulate matter and create its imaginings.

• We are matter created and animated by energy which moves through electromagnetic currents, sound and light to illuminate and animate matter. The interaction between light and matter determines the shape of everything we see. Sound affects us psychologically and electromagnetic currents gives motion to matter.

• Energy uses matter to not only express itself but to experience itself. In other words, energy and matter have a symbiotic relationship, revolve and evolve in space. However, matter and energy in our present physical form is at odds because matter in our form is conceptual and likes to take matters in its own hands developing an egoic intelligence which will do anything, including lie to itself and self-annihilate to be right.

• Energy is, at present, as far as our species is concerned, back on the drawing board for us to re-imagine ourselves and create harmony in symbiosis with matter because we matter to the universe and because we are the universe's kin.

Universal energy

Universal energy has symmetry, is reflective and communicates through moments of serendipity. Energy, matter and space are part of the reflective consciousness of the universe and that universal consciousness is reflecting in you and through you because you are the animated physical manifestation of that energy. We create with the power of that reflective energy consciousness with our thoughts, images and actions and what we create is reflected right back at us. That is the nature of the revolving symmetry of the reflective energy of the universe. The reason we don't easily make that connection is because it's like a long-distance relationship; there is a time delay in the manifestation of coming together in physical reality.

The saying 'good things come to those who wait' comes to mind.

When we become aware of that time delay, we then become aware of the consequences our thoughts, actions and images created in serendipitous energy. Serendipity, seemingly random, is reshaping and responding to our thoughts, images and actions, and will create events and opportunities according to the thoughts, images and actions of our belief systems.

The reason I bring up serendipity in this book is because it is part of a creative process, which seems random, unconnected and coincidental. However, so often with our thoughts, actions and intensions we unwarily tap into the ethereal universal energy around us to create the opportunities of our future. Being aware of the connection between ourselves, energy and serendipity, will lead to the union of ourselves, the universe and the endless possibilities, because we are all children of the universe.

Try being aware of your most dominant thoughts and become aware of events and situations which come your way – the time delay can be quick or it could take years depending on the clarity of your thoughts, your images, the driving emotional intensity and what it is you are trying to manifest. It's just like when you think of someone with some intensity, then they ring you or you bump into them – don't know about you but that sort of thing happens to me often. Start noticing this in all aspects of your life and after a while you will see what I mean.

The universe does not discriminate, it acts in reflection. That is why in our paradigm of duality we can manifest good or evil with that same universal energy. Because the universal consciousness does not discriminate, it is neither good nor evil. It just is! When that consciousness enters the physical realm, good and evil become a created concept creating duality by opposition and that separation keeps us trapped in discrimination and in opposition to the universal consciousness. This physical opposition is what we project back into the universal consciousness and what we are projecting and receiving back is triggered by our belief system.

Believing is not knowing, it is ego-based fabrication, whereas knowing comes from inner wisdom that is the wisdom of a non-discriminating universal consciousness. Nothing is random in the universe and we create what we receive, unfortunately, unwarily.

The choice is yours! Create with awareness or create as a victim?

The universal energy is part you and you are part of it and together we are on a journey to experience the magic of being in the form of animated physicality that is us and all other life.

Along the way on our journey, someone decided for us that life was not meant to be easy and instead of listening to ourselves we followed and created the world around us to be difficult. The huwoman knows that life is not meant to be difficult, it is meant to be appreciated – appreciate every moment of your life with kindness, thoughtful action, trust in yourself and you will move on-to the path of serendipity, the connecting and uniting aspect between you and universal energy.

When we are operating through the awareness of mind consciousness which is connected to the senses which in turn are connected to our surroundings and the universe, then thought is influenced by creative imagination rather than in the reactive thoughtlessness of our actions and fantasies towards what is around us. It is in the physical illusion of what we call time where we create and compose the poetic verse of our lives. This is the importance of thought awareness and thought images, as they are the seeds we plant to create our reality.

The universe unpacked = Uni – you one – Verse – the poetic language of universal energy.

You-thoughtful action-energy
You-thoughtful action-time
Thoughtful action-time-serendipity

This is an example of a trinity within a trinity within a trinity. All three aspects are connected, revolve and overlap at the same time and in numerological terms is housed in the number nine. One could also call this trinity the play between you, universal energy and the law of reflective attraction.

Creation as I see it

This is my take on creation and it may change as my awareness grows but I will attempt to explain and clarify what is difficult to put into words because it stems from my stream of consciousness.

Energy, space and matter are the fundamental building blocks of all that is and they are the trinity and the deity of our universe.

• When matter and energy combine they shape and create with light, sound and electromagnetic currents. When these physical structures disintegrate or die then all the properties used are recycled as part of the evolution of the universe.

• Because matter, energy and space cannot be created nor destroyed and only reshaped, the possibilities are endless.

• Energy creates shapes and manipulates according to the development and evolvement of the awareness of its imaginative intelligence. Its imaginative intelligence lives in its manifestation of animated matter, all animals, plants and inanimate matter are part of that active intelligence and contribute to its awareness to not only aid in its own evolution, but to also help the universe experience its consciousness. Without animated matter, the universe, the same as the unconscious us, just does what it does over and over again and its creative possibilities are not realised.

Energy needs physical animated vehicles in order to create more than its heavenly bodies.

While I don't like to use the word 'level' because it implies hierarchy, as the universe operates in a trinity, I wonder if levels of awareness did exist, they would be three, six or nine, that correspond with the trinity.

The editor in her wisdom replied to my question on levels of imagination in our existence:

> There may possibly be levels of imagination in existence, however, it is my understanding that the more light we are able to embody, the more attributes of our multidimensional being come into play. Therefore, our imagination has no beginning nor end, we simply are creation in our self-expression and the scope for that is unlimited.

∞

FINAL WORDS

We are evolving into a human who will not be able to live in the organic world making us dependent on a system based on artificiality which is resource hungry and finite – this system will stop at nothing and is devoid of genuine caring for our planet in its race for progress to line its pockets.

The Earth is not our enemy – she is life-giving and like us is a living breathing organism with a strong sense for survival. She does that by the balance of the elements and the biodiversity she houses. To continue to survive, she must address the continual damaging bombardment created by us. She is biodiverse and elemental and through her elements and her biodiversity she tries to balance. We experience her balancing act as tumultuous and threatening. Extreme tumultuous activity is the action necessary to keep herself and us alive for as long as she can, but we are too stupid to see this and instead of acting to help her to help ourselves we continue to bombard her from all levels with our carelessness, disrespect and pollute her with poisons and inorganic substances.

As a species, phenotypically speaking, we are female in origin. We must morph back into her psychologically if we have any chance of survival.

The huwomankind trinity is coming into being = woman-man-huwoman = hu/wo/man.

Though we do not recognise her yet, the huwoman lives deep inside our body, soul and spirit.

Soul is one's core of inner essence and that which fuels the physical.
Spirit is one's mind of imagination and driver of the physical.
Body is one's physical body which houses the soul and spirit.
All three together create our reality.

Body, soul, spirit is the trinity which connects us to the universe and makes us the universe. Rather than creating our planet into a death planet let's create her into the planet of life for our future survival as a species. Unfortunately, in this stepping stone evolution we are lacking in wisdom and that is reflected in the way we act towards our planet and everything that calls her home.

In the very likely case that we will cause an unnatural apocalypse, to continue to evolve as a species, hopefully enough will survive long enough for evolution to take its imaginative and kind hand to reinvent and project us into the highly evolved and civilised huwoman, for the continuation and longevity of our amazing species.

No matter what shape universal consciousness takes in the physical realm, it is a privilege to experience the magical world of being alive and it is necessary for creating a universe which is of consciousness. We, with plants and animals, are that consciousness of possibilities.

If we start to understand with the awareness that our consciousness can create, through our imagination, the possibilities are endless. The physical realm is to experience these possibilities. The physical world is always an illusion of our making created in the physical through the ethereal in the astral realm. The images we unwittingly and unwarily project create our own destiny and evolution. By starting to understand with our conscious awareness the possibilities that our imagination can create, we can then consciously be in control of our future evolutions from the imaginative life-giving trajectory instead of the destructive trajectory of our present fantasies.

You may call me a mad old crone and think that this whole book is a figment of my imagination, however it does not change the fact that it is another possible reality which can be created by us on earth if we think to and act to.

And maybe the wisdom of a whole lot of mad old crones is exactly what we need to lead us out of this crisis of disrespect for and disconnection from our planet, started by our forefathers thousands of years ago.

Let's face it, as humans we find it difficult to face ourselves and our primordial psychology. So, we create a detached, destructive and faceless system to reflect our inability to face ourselves and the reality of our making and that is the psychology of the CRAP system we have created and support.

The patriarchal images of our thoughts and actions act like sentinels guarding the entrance to the astral veil of ethereal light and what is possible beyond our present paradigm. The e-the-real astral light and beyond are the unknown and a place to create from a new. Let's bypass our sentinels and enter the veil with imaginative thinking, kindness, thoughtful actions and the will to create ourselves anew and in the huwoman's paradigm of peace.

The huwoman is the creation of our next evolution. Where she takes that evolution and what she takes it into is the unknown. However, she has the strength, the emotional wit and the ingenuity of both our female and male aspects in balance for survival.

The huwoman is offering a new image, and for her to come into being, we must start thinking and acting like her. Then we can change all those ancestral images that hover around us, shadowing our psychology.

Let's find it in ourselves to create in the psychology of the huwoman, where to be kind is to be kindred, to be kindred is to be connected. That is the primordial psychology of the huwoman.

Wow! We as a species are wonder woman! What a gift we are.
Let's act like that cherished gift and create the super-extraordinary
huwoman
as a present to ourselves.

Instead of living in a patriarchal **king-dom**, let's live in the **kind-dom** of the huwoman.

NICOLA SAGE GARDNER

I fill you with the light of love
I fill you with the energy of the sun
I fill you with de-light-full love
I fill you with to the brim with all that loving light.

Note: If someone reads this book in 100 years and finds themselves in Utopia, be aware, this was written in the 21st century and re-flects back through the ages to B.C.

ABOUT THE AUTHOR

Nicola Sage Gardner deeply cares for this Earth, our planet, our home. She grieves for her and does her best in this mad world to be gentle with her footprints. Nicola is an artist, philosopher and author. Her books are her gift to humanity for the sake of our planet.

Books – *Questions from a sometimes philosopher looking for utopia* and *Evolution of the sustainable huwoman.* Nicola's work in progress is *Huwoman Philosophy.*